10

22

25

D1232492

table of
contents

knitting for babies

knitting for kids

from the staff

Whether you are an avid, experienced knitter or just learning the basics, you'll be thrilled with these patterns for creating cute knitted projects for babies and kids.

The Knitting for Babies section includes soft, cuddly baby blankets, hats, and sweaters in pastels as well as a set that includes a blanket, sweater, and cap decorated with cute little mice—complete with whiskers and tails!

In the Knitting for Kids section, you'll find an easy-knit patchwork pullover and a cardigan knit in chunky rainbow yarn. In addition, one sweater includes intarsia flowers, another a car, and still another snaps several giant yarn posies over the front opening.

Whichever projects you choose, be sure to experiment with some of the fabulous yarns now available; check Knit Basics to learn more about substituting yarns.

Children and their parents will appreciate your thoughtfulness, whether you give a knitted project as a baby gift, a birthday or holiday present, or "just because."

happy knitting!

babies

Cuddle them, love them, and pamper them with handmade knit outfits made from touchably soft yarns. Babies will snuggle up and stay cozy warm in these sweet little sets.

pretty in pink

Any mother would be thrilled to see her baby girl wearing this adorable ensemble. A keyhole back opening in the dress allows for easy over-the-head dressing.

skill level: Experienced

sizes: 6 (12, 18) mos.
Instructions are written for the smallest size with changes for larger sizes given in parentheses. When only one number is given, it applies to all sizes.
Note: For ease in working, circle all numbers pertaining to the size you're knitting.

finished measurements
Dress:
Chest = 20 (20¹/₂, 22)"
Length = 16¹/₄ (18, 20³/₄)"
Cap:
Circumference = 16"
Cardigan:
Chest (buttoned) = 23 (25, 27)"
Length = 11 (12, 13)"

suggested yarn
Patons Bumblebee Baby Cotton
100% cotton; 1³/₄ oz. (50 g); 123 yds. (112 m); double-knitting (DK) weight
For Dress:
● 6 (6, 7) balls #2421 Apple Blossom
For Cap:
● 1 ball #2421 Apple Blossom
For Cardigan:
● 4 (4, 5) balls #2421 Apple Blossom

needles and extras
● Size 6 (4 mm) 36" circular knitting needle OR SIZE NEEDED TO OBTAIN GAUGE
● Size 3 (3.25 mm) 36" circular knitting needle
● Size 6 (4 mm) knitting needles OR SIZE NEEDED TO OBTAIN GAUGE
● Size 3 (3.25 mm) knitting needles
● Stitch holder
● Blunt-end yarn needle
● Size D/3 (3.25 mm) crochet hook
● Five ¹/₂"-diameter buttons (for Cardigan)
● One button (for Dress)

gauge
22 sts and 30 rows = 4" (10 cm) in St st using larger needles.
TAKE TIME TO CHECK YOUR GAUGE.

special abbreviations
Ssk (slip, slip, knit) = Slip next 2 stitches knitwise, one at a time to right-hand needle, insert tip of left-hand needle into fronts of these 2 stitches and knit 2 together.

MB (make bobble) = (Knit 1, yarn over, knit 1, yarn over, knit1) all in next stitch. Turn; knit 5. Turn; purl 5. Turn; knit 1, slip 1, knit 2 together, pass slipped stitch over, knit 1. Turn; purl 3 together—1 stitch remains.

MB2 (make bobble—double stitches) = Knit next 2 stitches together but do not slip stitches off needle. (Yarn over, knit same 2 stitches together again) twice. Slip stitches onto right-hand needle. Slip fourth, third, second, and first stitches separately over fifth stitch—1 stitch remains.

Sl 1 (slip 1) = Slip 1 stitch purlwise and with yarn on wrong side of fabric.

P2togb (purl 2 stitches together backward) = Turn work slightly, insert right-hand needle from left to right into 2nd and then first stitches and purl them together.

pattern stitches
CLIMBING VINE LACE PATTERN (a multiple of 11 sts; a 20-row rep)
Row 1 (RS): * K1, MB, k2, yo, k1, yo, k4, k2tog; rep from * across.
Rows 2, 4, 6, 8, and 10: *P2tog, p10; rep from * across.
Row 3: *K5, yo, k1, yo, k3, k2tog; rep from * across.
Row 5: *K6, yo, k1, yo, k2, k2tog; rep from * across.
Row 7: *K7, (yo, k1) twice, k2tog; rep from * across.
Row 9: *K8, yo, k1, yo, k2tog; rep from * across.
Row 11: *Ssk, k4, yo, k1, yo, k2, MB, k1; rep from * across.
Rows 12, 14, 16, and 18: *P10, p2togb; rep from * across.

Row 13: Ssk, k3, yo, k1, yo, k5; rep from * across.
Row 15: * Ssk, k2, yo, k1, yo, k6; rep from * across.
Row 17: * Ssk, (k1, yo) twice, k7; rep from * across.
Row 19: * Ssk, yo, k1, yo, k8; rep from * across.
Row 20: As Row 12.
Rep these 20 rows for the Climbing Vine Lace pat.

instructions
DRESS
front
**Beg at lower edge, and using smaller circular needle, cast on 110 (120, 130) sts. Do not join. Work back and forth across needle in rows as follows:
Edging Pattern
Row 1 (WS): Knit.
Rows 2–3: Knit.
Row 4: K1; *yo, MB2; rep from * to last st, k1.
Rows 5–6: Knit.
Row 7: Knit, inc 2 (3, 4) sts evenly across last row—112 (123, 134) sts. Using larger circular needle, work 2 rows in Garter st, then work in Climbing Vine Lace pat (working first and last st of each row in St st) until Front measures approx 10½ (11½, 13½)" from beg, ending with a WS row. Change to larger straight needles.
Next row: *K2tog; rep from * to last 0 (1, 0) st. K0 (1, 0)—56 (62, 67) sts.
Next row: Knit, dec 6 (10, 11) sts evenly across—50 (52, 56) sts.
Work 9 more rows in Garter st.
Next row (WS): Knit, inc 5 sts evenly across—55 (57, 61) sts.
Body Pattern
Row 1 (RS): K5 (3, 2); *yo, ssk, k5; rep from * to last 8 (5, 3) sts, yo, ssk, k6 (3, 1).
Rows 2–4: Work 3 rows even in St st.

Row 5: K1 (6, 5); *yo, ssk, k5; rep from * to last 5 (2, 7) sts, (yo, ssk) 1 (0, 1) time(s), k3 (2, 5).

Rows 6–8: Work 3 rows St st. Last 8 rows form Body pat. Work 2 (4, 6) more rows even in est pat.

Shape Armholes

Keeping pat as est, bind off 3 sts at beg of next 2 rows—49 (51, 55) sts. Dec 1 st each end of row on next and following alt rows until there are 45 (49, 49) sts**.

Work 3 (5, 7) rows even in pat, ending with a WS row.

Shape Neck

Next row: Work pat across 17 (19, 19) sts (neck edge). Turn. Leave rem sts on a spare needle. Work 1 row even in pat. Dec 1 st at neck edge on next and following alt rows until there are 9 (11, 11) sts. Work 1 row even in pat. Bind off. With RS facing, slip center 11 sts onto a st holder. Rejoin yarn to rem sts and work to correspond to other side.

back

Work as for Front from ** to **. Work 3 (5, 7) rows even in pat, ending with a WS row.

Back Opening

Next row: Work pat across 22 (24, 24) sts; bind off center st. Work pat to end of row. Working on right side of Back, work 11 rows even in pat.

Shape Neck

Next row (RS): Bind off 8 sts (neck edge). Work pat to end of row.

Dec 1 st at neck edge on next 5 rows—9 (11, 11) sts. Work 1 row even in pat. Bind off. With WS facing, rejoin yarn to left side of Back sts and work to correspond to right side, reversing all shapings.

finishing

Shape Armbands

Sew shoulder seams. With RS facing and using smaller needles, pick up and k40 (44, 48) sts along armhole edge. K 2 rows. Bind off kwise on WS.

Shape Back Edging

With RS facing and using smaller needles, pick up and k9 sts down right edge of Back opening, 1 st at center and 9 sts up left edge of Back opening—19 sts. Bind off kwise on WS.

Shape Neckband

With RS facing and using smaller needles, pick up and k13 sts up left neck edge of Back and 14 sts down left neck edge of Front. K11 from Front st holder, dec 1 st at center. Pick up and k14 sts up right neck edge of Front and 13 sts down right neck edge of Back—64 sts. K 3 rows.

Next row: K1, *yo, MB2. Rep from * to last st, k1. K 2 rows. Bind off kwise on WS. Sew side seams.

To make button loop (lp): With crochet hook, join yarn with a sl st in corner of right back neck. Ch 6, slip stitch at base of Garter st border; turn. Sc over ch-6 lp 10 times. Fasten off. Sew button to correspond to lp.

CAP

Using smaller needles, cast on 86 sts. Work 7 rows of Edging pat as for Front of Dress, inc 2 sts evenly across last row—88 sts. Work 2 rows in St st, then work 20 rows in Climbing Vine Lace pat. Work 2 rows in St st.

Shape Top

Row 1 (RS): *K2tog, k9; rep from * to end of row—80 sts.

Row 2 and all even rows: Purl.

Row 3: *K2tog, k8; rep from * to end of row—72 sts.

Row 5: *K2tog, k7; rep from * to end of row—64 sts. Cont in this manner, dec 8 sts evenly across every following alt row until there are 16 sts.

Next WS row: (P2tog) 8 times. Break yarn, leaving a long end. Draw end tightly through rem sts and fasten securely. Sew center back seam.

CARDIGAN

Set Up Body Pattern (worked in one piece to armholes)

Beg at lower edge and using smaller circular needle, cast on 120 (130, 140) sts. Do not join. Work back and forth across needle in rows. Rep Rows 1–6 of Edging pat as for Dress Front.

Row 7: Knit, inc 5 (6, 7) sts evenly across—125 (136, 147) sts. Using larger circular needle, work 2 rows in St st, then work in Climbing Vine Lace Pat (working first and last 2 sts of each row in St st) until Body measures approx 7 (7¾, 8¼)" from beg, ending with a WS row.

Shape Armholes

Next row: Work pat across 27 (30, 32) sts. Bind off next 8 (8, 9) sts. Cont in pat across 55 (60, 65) sts (including st on needle after bind-off). Bind off next 8 (8, 9) sts. Work pat to end of row.

Working on Left Front, work 1 row even in pat, then dec 1 st at the beg of the next and following alt rows 2 (3, 4) times more—24 (26, 27) sts. Work even in pat to approx 9 (10, 11)" from beg, ending with a RS row.

Shape Neck

Bind off 6 sts at beg of next row. Dec 1 st at neck edge on next and following alt rows until 13 (13, 14) sts rem. Work even in pat to approx 11 (12, 13)" from beg, ending with a WS row. Bind off.

back

With WS of work facing, rejoin yarn to center 55 (60, 65) sts. Work 1 row even in pat, then dec 1 st at each end of the next and following alt rows 2 (3, 4) times more—49 (52, 55) sts. Work even in pat to approx 11 (12, 13)" from beg, ending with a WS row. Bind off.

right front

With WS of work facing, rejoin yarn to last 27 (30, 32) sts. Work 1 row even in pat, then dec 1 st at end of the next and following alt rows 2 (3, 4) more times —24 (26, 27) sts. Work even in pat to approx 9 (10, 11)" from beg, ending with a WS row.

Shape Neck

Bind off 6 sts at beg of next row. Work 1 row even in pat, then dec 1 st at neck edge on next and following alt rows until there are 13 (13, 14) sts. Work even in pat to approx 11 (12, 13)" from beg, ending with a WS row. Bind off.

sleeve (make 2)

Beg at lower edge and using smaller straight needles, cast on 30 sts. Work 7 rows of Edging pat as for Dress Front, inc 1 st in center of last row—31 sts. Change to larger needles.

Set Up Body Pattern

Row 1 (RS): K4; * yo, ssk, k5; rep from * to last 6 sts, yo, ssk, k4.

Rows 2–4: Work 3 rows even in St st.

Row 5: K7; * yo, ssk, k5; rep from * to last 3 sts, yo, ssk, k1.

Rows 6–8: Work 3 rows in St st. Last 8 rows form Body pat. Cont in est pat, shaping sides by inc 1 st each edge on next and every 8th row 4 (5, 6) total times—39 (41, 43) sts. Work even to approx 6¼ (7½, 8¼)" from beg, ending with a WS row.

Shape Sleeve Cap

Cont in est pat, bind off 2 sts at beg of next 2 rows, then dec 1 st each end of next and every alt row until 19 sts rem. Dec 1 st at each end of every row until 13 sts rem. Bind off.

finishing

Sew shoulder and sleeve seams.

Make Buttonhole Band

With RS facing and using smaller needles, pick up and k46 (50, 56) sts evenly spaced from lower edge to neck edge along Right Front edge. K 1 row.

Row 2 (Buttonholes—RS): K2 (2, 3) sts. *Bind off 2 sts. K8 (9, 10) sts (including st on needle after bind off). Rep from * 3 times more. Bind off 2 sts. K to end of row.

Row 3: K, casting on 2 sts over bound-off sts.

Rows 4–5: Knit.

Bind off kwise on WS.

Shape Left Front Band

With RS facing and using smaller needles, pick up and k46 (50, 56) sts evenly spaced from neck edge to lower edge along Left Front edge. Work 5 rows in Garter st (knit every row). Bind off kwise on WS.

Make Collar

With RS facing and using smaller needles, pick up and k18 (20, 20) sts up Right Front neck edge (beg at center of side edge of Buttonhole Band). Pick up and k22 (24, 26) sts across center Back neck edge, then 18 (20, 20) sts down Left Front neck edge (ending at center of side edge of Button Band)—58 (64, 66) sts. Work approx 2 (2¼, 2¼)" in Garter st, ending with a WS row.

Next row (RS of Collar/WS of Cardigan): K1, *yo, MB2; rep from * to last st, k1. K 2 rows. Bind off knitwise on WS of Collar. Sew in Sleeves. Sew buttons opposite buttonholes.

Design by Gayle Bunn

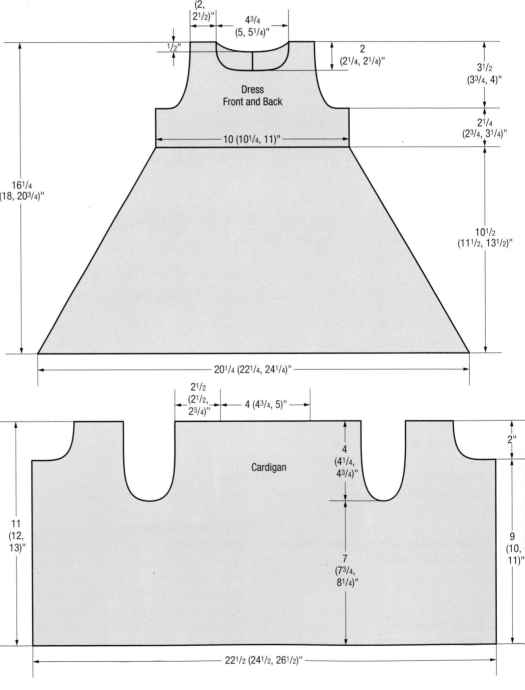

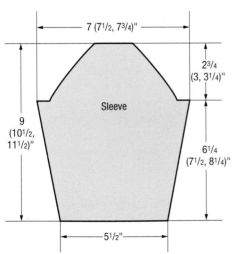

snuggle-up set

Keep baby toasty warm in a soft hooded pullover and matching drawstring pants. The X and O cable pattern is a subtle reminder that babies need lots of hugs and kisses.

skill level: Intermediate

sizes: 3–6 (6–12, 12–18) mos. Instructions are written for the smallest size with changes for larger sizes in parentheses. When only one number is given, it applies to all sizes.
Note: For ease in working, circle all numbers pertaining to the size you're knitting.

finished measurements
Sweater:
Chest = 22 (24, 27)"
Length = 10½ (11, 12)"
Pants:
Waist = 17½ (18, 20½)"
Length = 14 (16, 18)"

suggested yarn
Sandnes (Swedish Yarn Imports) Lanett 100% superwash merino wool; 1¾ oz. (50 g); 213 yds. (195 m); fingering weight
• 5 (5, 6) balls #5904 Baby Blue

needles & extras
• Size 3 (3.25 mm) knitting needles OR SIZE NEEDED TO OBTAIN GAUGE
• Size 2 (2.75 mm) knitting needles
• Cable needle
• Three stitch holders
• Blunt-end yarn needle

gauge
24 sts and 38 rows = 4" (10 cm) in St st using larger needles.
TAKE TIME TO CHECK YOUR GAUGE.

special abbreviations

K1B (knit 1 in row below) = Insert needle through center of stitch below next stitch on needle and knit this in the usual way, slipping the stitch above off the needle at the same time.

C4B (cable 4 at back) = Slip 2 stitches to circular needle and hold at back, knit 2; knit 2 from circular needle.

C4F (cable 4 in front) = Slip 2 stitches to circular needle and hold at front, knit 2; knit 2 from circular needle.

Sssk (slip, slip, slip, knit) = Slip next 3 stitches singly and knitwise to right-hand needle, insert tip of left-hand needle into fronts of these 3 stitches and knit them together.

pattern stitches

PATTERN A

RIB STITCH (over 17 sts; a 2-row rep)

Row 1 (RS): P1, k2, p1, k3, p1, k2, p1, k3, p1, k2.

Row 2: P2, K1B, p3, K1B, p2, K1B, p3, K1B, p2, K1B.

Rep Rows 1–2 for Pattern A.

PATTERN B

OXOX CABLE (panel of 12 sts; a 22-row rep)

Row 1 (RS): P2, C4B, C4F, p2.

Row 2 and all even-numbered (WS) rows: K the k sts and p the p sts.

Rows 3, 5, and 7: P2, k8, p2.

Row 9: P2, C4F, C4B, p2.

Row 11: P2, k8, p2.

Row 13: Rep Row 9.

Rows 15 and 17: P2, k8, p2.

Row 19: Rep Row 1.

Row 21: P2, k8, p2.

Row 22: Rep Row 2.

Rep Rows 1–22 for Pattern B.

PATTERN C

RIB STITCH (over 17 sts; a 2-row rep)

Row 1 (RS): K2, p1, k3, p1, k2, p1, k3, p1, k2, p1.

Row 2: K1B, p2, K1B, p3, K1B, p2, K1B, p3, K1B, p2.

Rep Rows 1–2 for Pattern C.

PATTERN D

RIB STITCH (over 12 sts; 2-row rep)

Row 1 (RS): P1, k3, p1, k2, p1, k3, p1.

Row 2: K1B, p3, K1B, p2, K1B, p3, K1B.

Rep Rows 1–2 for Pattern C.

instructions
SWEATER
back

Beg at lower edge and using smaller needles, cast on 66 (74, 82) sts.

Ribbing

Row 1 (WS): P2; (k2, p2) across.

Row 2: K2; (p2, k2) across.

Rep Ribbing Rows 1–2 to approx 1" from beg, ending with a RS row. Change to larger needles and p 1 row.

Next row: K10 (14,18), work Pat A over 17 sts, Pat B over 12 sts, and Pat C over 17 sts, k10 (14, 18). Cont est pats to approx 6 (6½, 7)" from be; end with a WS row.

Shape Raglan

Bind off 6 sts at beg of next 2 rows—54 (62, 70) sts.

Dec row (RS): K2, k3tog, work est pat across to last 5 sts, sssk, k2. Rep Dec row every 4th row 7 (9, 11) more times—22 sts rem. Place marker on each edge to note start of hood panel.

Shape Back Hood Panel

Cont in est pat on rem sts for approx 9 (9, 10)", ending with a RS row. Rep Ribbing Rows 1–2 as for Back for approx 1", ending with a WS row. Bind off kwise.

front

Work as for Back to approx 8½ (10, 11)" from beg, ending with a WS row. Place markers (pm) on both sides of center 12 sts.

Shape Neck

Work in est pat to marker, place 12 sts on holder, join second ball of yarn and work to end of row. Working sides separately and AT THE SAME TIME, dec 1 st at each neck edge every other row 3 times. AT THE SAME TIME, work raglan shaping on following fourth rows as est until 2 sts rem. Cont in pat on rem 2 sts to approx 9½ (11, 12¼)" from beg, ending with a WS row. Bind off.

sleeve (make 2)

Beg at lower edge and using smaller needles, cast on 34 (34, 42) sts. Rep Ribbing as for Back to approx 1" from beg, ending with a RS row and AT THE SAME TIME inc 6 sts evenly spaced across last row—40 (40, 48) sts. Change to larger needles and p 1 row.

Next row: K14 (14, 18), work Pat D on 12 sts, k14 (14, 18). Pat is now set. Including new sts into St st side panels, beg with the next RS row, inc 1 st at each edge now, and then every 6th row 4 more times—50 (50, 58) sts. Work even to approx 6 (6, 7½)" from beg, ending with a WS row.

Shape Raglan

Bind off 6 sts at beg of next 2 rows—38 (38, 46) sts.

Dec row (RS): K2, k3tog, work pat across to last 5 sts, sssk, k2. Rep Dec row every 4th row 3 (0, 0) times, every 6th row 3 (6, 3) times, every 8th row 0 (0, 3) times. Work even on rem 10 (10, 18) sts to approx 9½ (10½, 12¾)" from beg, ending with a WS row. Place sts on holder.

finishing

Join Sleeves to Front and Back. Join side seams.

right hood side panel

With the RS facing and using larger needles, and beg at center Front neck edge, pick up and k4 sts across center cable plus 9 more sts evenly spaced up the right Front neck edge, k across 10 (10, 18) sts from Sleeve holder—23 (23, 31) total sts.

Next row: Purl.

Next row: P4, k to end.
Next row: Purl.
Next row: Knit. Rep last 4 rows for side panel and AT THE SAME TIME inc 1 st at Back edge every other row 6 times—29 (29, 37) sts.

Cont in est pat to approx 6 (6, 7)" from beg, ending with a WS row. Bind off loosely.

left hood side panel

K across 10 (10, 18) sts from Sleeve holder, pick up and k13 sts evenly spaced along left Front neck edge, ending with last 4 sts meeting at center Front neck. Reversing shaping and front border trim, work as for Right Hood Side Panel.

finishing

Join hood side panels to hood center. Without touching iron to fabric, steam lightly to finish.

PANTS
leg (make 2)

Beg at lower edge and using smallest needles, cast on 46 (50, 58) sts. Work 1" of Ribbing as for Sweater Back, ending with a RS row and inc 6 sts evenly spaced across last row—52 (56, 64) sts. Change to larger needles and p 1 row.

Body Pattern

Row 1 (RS): K3 (5, 9), work Pat A on 17 sts, Pat B on 12 sts, Pat C on 17 sts, k3 (5, 9). Pat is now est.

Next RS row: Including new sts into St st, inc 1 st at each edge now, and then every 12th row 4 more times —62 (66, 74) sts. Work even to approx 7½ (8½, 9½)" from beg, ending with a WS row.

Shape Crotch

Bind off 3 sts at beg of next 2 rows—56 (60, 68) sts. Dec 1 st at each edge every other row 3 times—50 (54, 62) sts. Cont in pat to approx 13 (15, 17)" from beg, ending with a RS row.

Make Trim

Changing to smaller needles, work ribbing as follows:
Row 1 (WS): P2; (k2, p2) across.
Row 2: K2; (p2, k2) across.
Rep Rows 1–2 to approx 14 (16, 18)" from beg, ending with a WS row. Bind off kwise.

i-cord

With smaller needles, cast on 3 sts.
Row 1: K3.
Row 2: Do not turn; slide the 3 sts to opposite end of needle. With working yarn at left end of stitches, take to back and k3.

Rep Row 2 until cord measures approx 20 (22, 24)" from beg. Bind off.

Join crotch and leg seams. Lace I-cord through center of waistband ribbing, and tie. Without touching iron to fabric, lightly steam to finish.

Design by Dawn Oertel

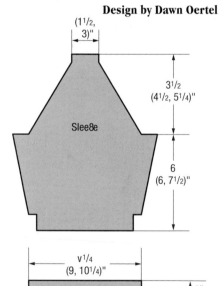

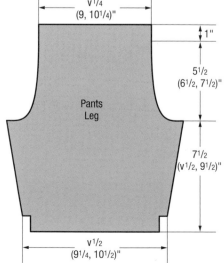

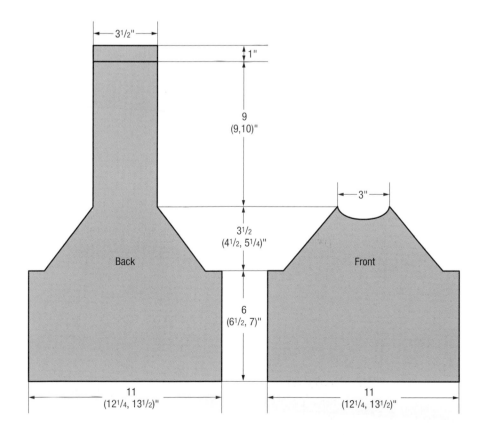

orange cardigan & jumper

The cardigan in this set is worked in one piece to the armholes. Tiny buttons accent the jumper at the shoulders. The softness of the cotton yarn makes the outfit a favorite for a little one to wear.

skill level: Intermediate

sizes: 6 (12, 18) mos.
Instructions are written for the smallest size with changes for larger sizes given in parentheses. When only one number is given, it applies to all sizes.
Note: For ease in working, circle all numbers pertaining to the size you're knitting.

finished measurements
Cardigan:
Chest = 19½ (22, 25)"
Length = 10½ (12, 13½)"
Upper arm = 9½ (10½, 12)"
Jumper:
Chest = 19 (20, 23)"
Length = 14½ (16½, 18½)"

suggested yarns
Patons Grace (Art. 246060)
100% cotton; 1¾ oz. (50 g); 136 yds (124 m); sport weight

For Cardigan:
- 3 (3, 4, 4) balls #60604 Terracotta (MC)
- 1 ball #60005 Snow (A)
- 1 ball #60437 Rose (B)
For Jumper:
- 2 (2, 3, 3) balls #60604 Terracotta (MC)
- 1 ball #60005 Snow (A)
- 1 ball #60437 Rose (B)

needles & extras
- Size 5 (3.75 mm) 24" circular knitting needles OR SIZE NEEDED TO OBTAIN GAUGE
- Size 4 (3.5 mm) 24" circular knitting needles
- Size 5 (3.75 mm) knitting needles
- Size 4 (3.5 mm) knitting needles
- Blunt-end yarn needle
- Five ½"-diameter buttons (for Cardigan)
- Two ½"-diameter buttons (for Jumper)
- Two snaps

gauge
24 sts and 32 rows = 4" in St st using larger needles.
TAKE TIME TO CHECK YOUR GAUGE.

instructions

CARDIGAN
Note: Body is worked in one piece to armholes.

body
Using smaller circular needle and B, cast on 113 (127, 147) sts. Work back and forth in rows as follows.
Row 1: (WS) Knit.
Change to larger needle.
Row 2: With A, knit.
Row 3: With A, p1; *p2 MC, p2 A; rep from * to last 0 (2, 2) sts, with MC, p0 (2, 2).
Row 4: With MC, p0 (2, 2); *k2 A, p2 MC; rep from * to last st, with A, k1.
Row 5: With A, purl.
Rows 6–7: With B, knit.
Next row: Changing to MC and beg with a knit row, work in St st until piece from beg measures 2¾ (3¾, 4½)", ending with a p row. Work Rows 1–22 of chart, *page 12,* reading from right to left for RS and from left to right for WS. Rep sts 1–12 across, ending last rep at st 17 (19, 15) for first RS row.

Shape Armholes
Next row: With MC, k24 (27, 30), bind off next 8 (10, 14) sts, k49 (53, 59) (including st on needle after bind off), bind off next 8 (10, 14) sts, k to end.

left front
Cont on last 24 (27, 30) sts, purl 1 row. Dec 1 st at Front edge on next and following RS rows until 15 (16, 19) sts rem, then on every 4th row until 12 (13, 15) sts rem. Cont even until armhole measures 4¾ (5¼, 6)", ending with a p row. Bind off.

back
With WS facing, join MC to rem sts and p49 (53, 59). Cont even until armhole measures same length as Left Front, ending with a p row.
Shape Shoulders
Bind off 12 (13, 15) sts at beg of next 2 rows. Place rem 25 (27, 29) sts on a st holder.

right front
With WS facing, join MC to rem 24 (27, 30) sts and work to correspond to Left Front, reversing all shaping.

sleeve (make 2)

With B and smaller needles, cast on 43 (47, 47) sts.

Row 1: (WS) Knit. Change to larger needles.

Row 2: With A, knit.

Row 3: With A, p1; * p2 MC, p2 A; rep from * to last 2 sts; p2 MC.

Row 4: * P2 MC, k2 A; rep from * to last 3 sts; p2 MC, k1 A.

Row 5: With A, purl.

Rows 6–7: With B, knit.

Next row: Change to M and beg with a knit row, work 4 rows St st.

Inc 1 st each end of next row and following 6th (6th, 4th) rows 5 (3, 6) more times, then on following 0 (8th, 6th) rows 0 (3, 5) more times—(61, 71) sts. Cont even until Sleeve from beg measures 7 (8, 9½)", ending with a purl row. Bind off. Place markers on side edges of sleeves ½ (¾, 1)" down from bound-off edge.

Finish Sleeves

Sew shoulder seams.

Make Neck Edging

With RS facing and using A and smaller circular needle, and beg at lower corner of Right Front, pick up and k33 (37, 41) sts up Right Front edge to first Front dec, k30 (33, 37) sts up Right Front neck edge, k25 (27, 29) from Back neck edge, dec 2 sts evenly across, pick up and k30 (33, 37) sts down Left Front neck edge to first Front dec and k33 (37, 41) sts down Left Front edge—149 (165, 183) sts. Knit 3 rows.

Next row (RS—buttonhole row): K3; * bind off 2 sts, k5 (6, 7) (including st on needle after bind-off); rep from * 3 more times, bind off 2 sts, k to end—5 buttonholes.

Next row: K, casting on 2 sts over bound-off sts.

Next row: With MC, k 1 row.

Bind off kwise on WS.

finishing

Set in Sleeves, placing rows above markers along bound-off sts at armholes to form square armholes. Sew Sleeve seams. Sew buttons opposite buttonholes.

JUMPER
back

Using B and smaller needles, cast on 77 (85, 97) sts.

Row 1 (WS): Knit.

Change to larger needles.

Row 2: With A, knit.

Row 3: With A, p1; *p2 MC, p2 A; rep from * to end.

Row 4: *K2 A, p2 MC; rep from * to last st; with A, k1.

Row 5: With A, purl.

Rows 6–7: With B, knit.

Next row: Change to MC and beg with a knit row, work 6 rows in St st.

Dec 1 st at each end of next and following 6th rows 6 (8, 10) more times—63 (67, 75) sts.

Work 3 rows even, ending with a WS row.

Work Rows 1–22, from Chart *below,* reading from right to left for RS and from left to right for WS, Rep sts 1–12 across, ending last rep at st 15 (19, 15) for first RS row. AT THE SAME TIME, dec 1 st at each edge on Rows 3, 9, and 15—57 (61, 69) sts.

Shape Armholes

Change to MC only and bind off 3 (4, 5) sts at beg of next 2 rows—51 (53, 59) sts.

Place Dot Pattern

Row 1 (RS): K2tog, k5 (0-0); *k1 A, k5 MC; rep from * to last 2 (3, 3) sts; k0 (1, 1) A, k2tog MC—49 (51, 57) sts.

Row 2: With MC, p.

Row 3: K2tog, k to last 2 sts; k2tog—47 (49, 55) sts.

Row 4: P2 (3, 3); *p1 A, p5 MC; rep from * to last 3 (4, 4) sts; p1 A, p2 (3, 3) MC.

Row 5: With MC, k2tog, k to last 2 sts; k2tog—45 (47, 53) sts.

Row 6: Purl.

Dot pat is now in position.

Size 18 months only: Cont in Dot pat, dec 1 st at each end of next row.

Other sizes [45 (47, 51) sts **]: Cont even in dot pat until armhole measures 3½ (4, 4¾)", ending with a p row.

Shape Back Neck

Next row (RS): Work pat across 15 sts (neck edge); turn. Leave rem sts on a spare needle. Dec 1 st at neck edge of next 4 rows—11 sts.

Cont even in pat until armhole measures 4½ (5, 5¼)", ending with a purl row. Place markers at each end of last row.

Shape Strap Extensions

Work 4 rows even in pat. Decrease 1 st at each end of next and following alt rows twice more. Bind off rem 5 sts.

With RS facing, sl center 15 (17, 21) sts onto a stitch holder. Rejoin yarn to rem 15 sts and work to correspond to other side, reversing all shaping.

front

Work from ** to ** as for Back. Cont even in Dot pat until armhole measures 2¼ (2¾, 2¾)", ending with a purl row.

Shape Front Neck

Next row (RS): Work pat across 17 (17, 18) sts (neck edge); turn. Leave rem sts on a spare needle. Dec 1 st at neck edge of next 4 rows, then on every RS row 2 (2, 3) times—11 sts. Cont even in pat until armhole measures 4 (4½, 5¼)", ending with a purl row. Bind off. With RS facing, sl center 11 (13, 15) sts onto a st holder. Rejoin yarn to rem 17 (17, 18) sts and work to correspond to other side, reversing all shaping. Sew side seams.

Make Armhole and Strap Edging

With RS facing and using smaller circular needle and A, beg at top corner of right armhole, pick up and k24 (27, 31) sts to side seam, k28 (31, 35) sts up Back side of armhole to marker, k27 sts around curved end of strap to opposite marker, k7 sts down right Back neck edge, k15 (17, 21) from Back st holder, dec 2 sts evenly across, pick up and k7 sts up left Back neck edge to marker, k27 sts around curved end of strap to opposite

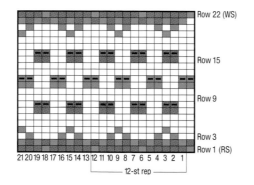

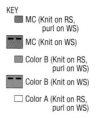

KEY

■ MC (Knit on RS, purl on WS)

▬ MC (Knit on WS)

■ Color B (Knit on RS, purl on WS)

▬ Color B (Knit on WS)

□ Color A (Knit on RS, purl on WS)

Row 22 (WS)

Row 15

Row 9

Row 3
Row 1 (RS)

21 20 19 18 17 16 15 14 13 12 11 10 9 8 7 6 5 4 3 2 1

12-st rep

marker, k28 (31, 35) sts down Back side of armhole to side seam and k24 (27, 31) sts up Front side of armhole —185 (199, 219) sts. Bind off kwise on WS.

Make Front Neck Edging

With RS facing and using A and smaller needles, beg at neck edge corner of left shoulder, pick up and k13 (13, 15) sts down Left Front neck edge, k11 (13, 15) from Front stitch holder, dec 2 sts evenly and pick up and k13 (13, 15) sts up Right Front neck edge to shoulder—35 (37, 43) sts. Bind off kwise on WS.

finishing

Sew buttons to Back strap extensions. Sew snaps in position on WS of back strap extension (under button) and RS of front shoulder.

Design by Gayle Bunn

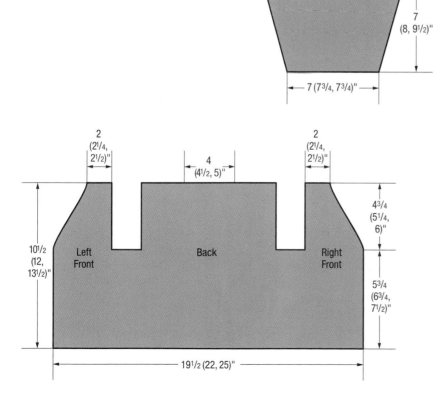

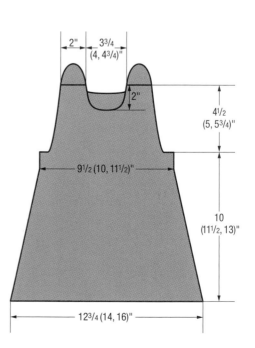

skill level: Intermediate

sizes: Cardigan: 12 (18, 24) mos.
Hat: One size fits most.
Instructions are written for the smallest size with changes for larger sizes given in parentheses. When only one number is given, it applies to all sizes.
Note: For ease in working, circle all numbers pertaining to the size you're makng.

finished measurements
Blanket:
30×34"
Cardigan:
Chest (buttoned) = 24 (25, 26)."
Hat:
Circumference = 17"

suggested yarns
Lion Brand Cotton-Ease (Art. 700)
50% cotton, 50% acrylic; 3½ oz. (100 g); 207 yds. (188 m); worsted weight
For Blanket:
• 3 balls #107 Candy Blue (MC)
• 3 balls #100 Vanilla (A)
For Cardigan and Hat:
• 2 (3, 3) balls #107 Candy Blue (MC)
• 1 (1, 2) balls #100 Vanilla (A)

Lion Brand Wool-Ease (Art. 620)
80% acrylic, 20% wool; 197 yds. (180 m); 3 oz. (85 g); worsted weight
For Blanket:
• 1 ball #151 Grey Heather (B)
For Cardigan and Hat:
• 1 ball #151 Grey Heather (B)

needles & extras
• Size 8 (5 mm) 29" circular needle OR SIZE NEEDED TO OBTAIN GAUGE
• Size 6 (4 mm) knitting needles (for Cardigan and Hat only)
• Stitch holders (for Cardigan only)
• 1½ yds. thin tubular white elastic (whiskers)
• Six ⅜"-diameter white two-hole dome buttons (for eyes on Blanket only)
• Three ⅜"-diameter white two-hole dome buttons (for eyes on Cardigan only)
• Four (four, five) ½"-diameter white half-ball buttons with shank (for Cardigan only)
• Blunt-end yarn needle
• Small crochet hook (for embellishments)

gauge
18 sts and 24 rows = 4" (10 cm) in St st using larger needle.
TAKE TIME TO CHECK YOUR GAUGE.

mouse baby set

This darling set features wooly mice with dimensional features—tails, eyes, ears, and even whiskers.

instructions

BLANKET

Notes: This blanket is worked in one piece going back and forth using a circular needle. Work each Block with a separate ball of yarn. Twist yarn on WS to prevent holes. Embellish the mice when blanket is complete.

blocks

Each block is worked in St st with 30 sts and 36 rows as follows:

Solid Blocks

Rows 1–36: MC or A (as shown in diagram, *right*).

Striped Block 1

Rows 1–4: MC.
Rows 5–8: A.
Rows 9–32: Rep Rows 1–8 three more times.
Rows 33–36: MC.

Striped Block 2

Rows 1–4: A.
Rows 5–8: MC.
Rows 9–32: Rep Rows 1–8 three more times.
Rows 33–36: A.

Mouse-Face Blocks (See Chart #1, *page 16.*)

Rows 1–8: MC.
Row 9: K 13 sts in MC; join B and work Chart #1 over next 4 sts, end k 13 sts in MC.
Rows 10–24: Cont working Chart #1.
Rows 25–36: MC.

Mouse-Body Blocks (See Chart #2, *page 16.*)

Rows 1–12: MC.
Row 13: K 7 sts in MC; join B and work Chart #2 over next 15 sts, end k 8 sts in MC.
Rows 14–23: Cont working Chart #2.
Rows 24–36: MC.

Dot Block 1

Rows 1–2: MC.
Rows 3–4: 2 MC, *2 A, 4 MC; rep from * 3 more times; 2 A, 2 MC.
Rows 5–8: MC.
Rows 9–10: 5 MC, *2 A, 4 MC; rep from * 3 more times; end 1 MC.
Rows 11–12: MC.
Rows 13–36: Rep Rows 1–12 twice more.

Dot Block 2 (Refer to Dot Block 1 Chart on *page 16,* working A for MC, and MC for A.)

Rows 1–2: A.
Rows 3–4: 2 A, *2 MC, 4 A; rep from * 3 more times; 2 MC, 2 A.
Rows 5–8: A.

Rows 9–10: 5 A, *2 MC, 4A; rep from * 3 more times; end 1 A.
Rows 11–12: A.
Rows 13–36: Rep Rows 1–12 twice more.

blanket pattern

Using circular needle and MC, cast on 128 sts. Work in Garter st (k every row) for 1".

Next Row (RS): Work 4 sts in Garter st for border in MC, then join in new balls of yarn as necessary and work 4 blocks of 30 sts, referring to Blanket Assemby Diagram, *right*; join separate ball of MC yarn and work 4 st in Garter st for border. Working Garter st borders along both edges of blanket, cont to follow instructions and refer to Blanket Assembly Diagram, until all blocks are complete. With MC, work in Garter st for 1". Bind off.

Make Eyes, Ears, Whiskers, and Tails

Follow instructions as for Cardigan, page 16.

CARDIGAN
back

Using smaller needles and MC, cast on 54 (56, 58) sts. Work in k1, p1 rib for 8 rows. Change to circular needle and work in St st for 2 rows.

Next row (RS): K2 (3, 4) MC, join A, *k2 A, k4 MC; rep from * across, ending k2 (3, 4) MC.
Next row: P2 (3, 4) MC, *p2 A, p4 MC; rep from * across, ending p2 (3, 4) MC. Work 2 rows MC.
Next row: K5, (6, 7) MC, *k2 A, k4 MC; rep from * across row, ending k2 A, k5 (6, 7) MC.
Next row: P5, (6, 7) MC, *p2 A, p4 MC; rep from * across row, ending p2 A, p5 (6, 7) MC. Work even until piece measures 11 (12, 12¾)" from beg, ending with RS row.

Shape Back Neck (WS)

Bind off 16 (17, 18) sts; work across center 22 sts and place on holder; bind off rem 16 (17, 18) sts.

left front

Using smaller needles and MC, cast on 26 (26, 28) sts. Work in k1, p1 rib for 8 rows, inc 0 (1, 0) st in center of last row—26 (27, 28) sts. Change to circular needle and work in St st for 2 rows.

Next row (RS): K3 (4, 4) MC, join A, *k2 A, k4 MC; rep from * across, ending k2 A, k3 (3, 4) MC.
Next row: P3 (3, 4) MC, *k2 A, k4 MC; rep from * across, ending k3 (4, 4) MC. Work 2 rows MC.
Next row: K6 (7, 7) MC, *k2 A, k4 MC; rep from * across, ending k2 A, k6 (6, 7) MC.
Next row: P6 (6, 7) MC, *k2 A, k4 MC; rep from * across ending K6 (7, 7) MC. Work 2 rows MC.
Next row: K11 (12, 12) MC, join B and work Chart

#1, *page 16,* over next 4 sts, end k11 (11, 12) MC. Cont working in St st over 16 rows of Chart #1. Work even until piece measures 8½ (9½, 10¼)" from beg, ending with a RS row.

Shape Neck

Bind off 4 sts at neck edge. Cont to bind off at neck edge 2 sts twice, then 1 st twice—16 (17, 18) sts rem. Work even until piece measures 11 (12, 12¾)" from beg. Bind off.

right front

Work same as for Left Front until ready for chart.

Next row: K5 (5, 6) MC; join B and work Chart #2 over next 15 sts, end k6 (7, 7) MC. Cont working in St st over 11 rows of Chart #2. Complete as for Left Front, reversing neck shaping.

sleeve (make 2)

Using smaller needles and MC, cast on 30 (32, 34) sts. Work in k1, p1 rib for 8 rows, inc 4 sts evenly spaced across last row—34 (36, 38) sts.
Change to larger needles and A. Work Stripe pat as follows: *Work 4 rows A, work 4 rows MC; rep from * for length of sleeve. AT THE SAME TIME, inc 1 st at each edge every 6th row 6 times—46 (48, 50) sts. Cont even until piece measures 8 (8½, 9¾)" from beg. Bind off loosely.

finishing

Sew shoulder seams.

Blanket Assembly Diagram

Shape Neckband

With RS facing and using smaller needles and MC, pick up and k58 (60, 60) sts around neck edge. Work in k1, p1 rib for 7 rows. Bind off loosely.

Shape Button Band

With RS facing and using smaller needles and MC, pick up and k55 (58, 62) sts along Right Front edge (for boy) or Left Front edge (for girl). Work in k1, p1 rib for 7 rows. Bind off loosely.

Shape Buttonhole Band

With RS facing and using smaller needles and MC, pick up and k 55 (58, 62) sts along Right Front edge (for girl) or Left Front edge (for boy). Work 2 rows in k1, p1 rib.

Buttonhole row (WS): Work 4 sts in rib, *bind off 2 sts, work 13 (14, 11) sts in rib; rep from * 2 (2, 3) times, bind off 2 sts, work 4 sts in rib—4 (4, 5) buttonholes.

Next row: Work 4 sts in rib, *cast on 2 sts over bound-off sts, work 13 (14, 11) sts in rib; rep from * 2 (2, 3) times, cast on 2 sts, work 4 sts in rib. Work 2 more rows in rib. Bind off. Mark front and back edges 5¼ (5½, 5¾)" from shoulder seams. Attach Sleeves between markers. Sew side and underarm seams. Sew on half-ball buttons.

mouse face

Refer to Chart #1, *below center, top.*

For whiskers: Cut two 4½" strips from elastic and make knot at each end 3" apart. Crisscross the two pieces in center and sew tog with thread (to form X), then tack down onto fabric at nose location. With 1 strand of MC, satin-stitch a nose on top of crossed elastic, leaving whiskers loose.

For eyes: Following chart, sew on two dome button eyes with white thread.

For ears (make 2): Referring to X on chart, tack down a long strand of B. With small crochet hook, ch 20 with strand. Wind the ch-20 clockwise to form solid circle; tack the circle at various points to hold shape. The ears are loose except at points of attachment (X).

mouse body

Refer to Chart #2, *below middle, center.*

For tail: Following the chart, tack down a long strand of B. With a small crochet hook, work a 2½" ch, knot end, and leave loose.

For eye: Following the chart, attach dome-button eye with white thread.

For ear: Work as for Mouse Face: Chart #1.

HAT

Note: The hat is worked flat, then seamed.
Using smaller needles and MC, cast on 72 sts. Work in k1, p1 rib for 8 rows. Change to circular needle and work 2 rows in St st.

Next row (RS): K2 MC, join A, *k2 A, k4 MC; rep from * across, ending k2 A, k2 MC.

Next row: P2 MC, join in A, *p2 A, p4 MC; rep from * across, ending p2 A, p2 MC. Work 2 rows MC.

Next row: K4 MC, join in B and *work Chart #3, *below middle, bottom,* over next 11 sts, k6 MC; rep from * across row.

Cont working in St st over 8 rows of chart. Work even in MC until piece measures 4¼" from beg, ending with a WS row.

Shape Crown

Row 1: *K8, k2tog; rep from * 6 more times, end k2—65 sts.

Row 2 (WS) and all even-numbered rows: Purl.

Row 3: *K7, k2tog; rep from * 6 more times, end k2—58 sts.

Row 5: *K6, k2tog; rep from * 6 more times, end k2—51 sts.

Row 7: *K5, k2tog; rep from * 6 more times, end k2—44 sts.

Row 9: *K4, k2tog; rep from * 6 more times, end k2—37 sts.

Row 11: *K3, k2tog; rep from * 6 more times, end k2—30 sts.

Row 13: (K2tog) 15 times. Cut yarn, leaving 15" strand. Thread strand through sts and pull tightly. Sew seam.

mouse body (chart #3)

For tail: Following chart and using long strand of B and small crochet hook, attach at back end and work 1½" ch. Knot end and leave loose.

For eye: Following Chart #3 and using one strand of A, make French knot.

For ear: Work as for Cardigan Mouse Face: Chart #1, working 12 sts to make chain.

Design by Amy Bahrt

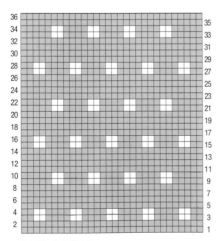

Dot Block 1 Chart

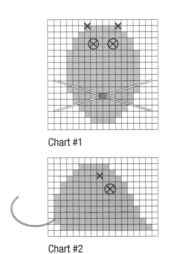

Chart #1

Chart #2

Chart #3

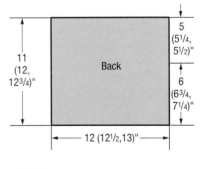

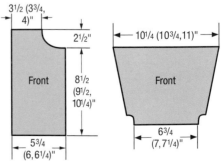

beribboned set

A twisted garter stitch and dimpled eyelet give this layette set soft detailing. Woven ribbon ties provide a practical and pretty closure to the sweater and hat; the booties also have a ribbon-closure option.

skill level: Intermediate

sizes: Cardigan: 6 (12, 18) mos.
Hat and Booties: One size fits all.
Instructions are written for the smallest size with changes for larger sizes given in parentheses. When only one number is given, it applies to all sizes.
Note: *For ease in working, circle all numbers pertaining to the size you're knitting.*

finished measurements
Sweater:
Chest (snapped) = 19½ (22, 24¾)"
Length = 10 (11, 12)"
Upper arm = 7¾ (8¾, 9¾)"

Hat:
Circumference = 14 (16)"
Booties:
Foot circumference = 3½"
Foot length = 2¾"

suggested yarn
Plymouth Encore DK
75% acrylic, 25% wool; 1¾ oz (50 g); 150 yds. (137 m); double-knitting (DK) weight
• 4 balls #896 Yellow

needles & extras
• Size 5 (3.75 mm) 24" circular knitting needle OR SIZE NEEDED TO OBTAIN GAUGE
• Size 5 (3.75 mm) 16" circular knitting needle

• Size 5 (3.75 mm) double-pointed needles (dpns)
• Stitch markers
• Stitch holders
• Blunt-end yarn needle
• Snap
• 4 yds (3.5 m) grosgrain ribbon, ⅜" (35 cm) wide

gauge
24 sts and 32 rows = 4" in St st using larger needles.
TAKE TIME TO CHECK YOUR GAUGE.

special abbreviations

Ssk (slip, slip, knit) = Slip next 2 stitches knitwise, one.at a time to right-hand needle, insert tip of left-hand needle into fronts of these 2 stitches and knit 2 together.

Yo (yarn over) = Take yarn back between needles, then wrap yarn over right-hand needle.

pattern stitches
TWISTED GARTER STITCH

All rows are knit through the back loop of every stitch.

DIMPLE EYELET (worked flat)

Row 1(RS): P1; *p2tog, yo; rep from *, end p1.
Row 2: P, purling through the back of each yo.
Row 3: Knit.
Row 4: Purl.
Row 5: Rep Row 1.
Row 6: Rep Row 2.

DIMPLE EYELET (worked in the round)

Rnds 1 and 5: *P2tog, yo; rep from *.
Rnds 2 and 6: K, knitting through the back of each yo.
Rnds 3 and 4: Knit.

instructions
CARDIGAN

Beg at the neck with circular needle, cast on 52 (56, 60) sts. Work back and forth without joining into a round. P across next row and place markers (pm) as follows: P3, pm, p11 (12, 13), pm, p24 (26, 28), pm, p11 (12, 13), pm, p3.

Shape Raglan

Setup row: Inc in first 2 sts, k1; *inc in next st, k to 2 sts before marker, inc, k1; rep from * twice more, inc in next 2 sts, k1 —62 (66, 70) sts. P 1 row.

Rows 1 and 3: Inc in first st; *k to 2 sts before marker, inc, k1, inc; rep from * 3 times more, k to last st, inc in last st—10 sts increased on each row.

Rows 2 and 4: Purl.

Row 5: Cable cast on (see Knit Basics, page 45) 8 (9, 10) sts at the beg of the row; * k to 2 sts before marker, inc, k1, inc; rep from * 3 times more, k to end of row—98 (103, 108) sts.

Row 6: Cable cast on 12 (13, 14) sts at the beg of the row, p across, working last 4 sts in Twisted Garter pat—110 (116, 122) sts.

Row 7: Work first 4 sts in Twisted Garter pat; *k to 2 sts before marker, inc, k1, inc; rep from * 3 times more, k to last 4 sts, work Twisted Garter pat—118 (124, 130) sts.

Keeping first and last 4 sts in Twisted Garter pat, cont in St st and raglan shaping until you have 56 (62, 68) sts between the Back markers and 206 (228, 250) total sts, ending with a WS row.

Divide for Body and Sleeves

Keeping first and last 4 sts in Twisted Garter pat throughout, remove all raglan markers as you work. Cont pat to first marker, place next 43 (48, 53) sts on waste yarn for Sleeve, cast on 4 (4, 6) sts onto the right tip of the needle, k to next marker, place next 43 (48, 53) sts on waste yarn for Sleeve, cast on 4 (4, 6) sts onto the right needle tip, k to end of row—128 (140, 156) body sts.

body

Work even to 2¼ (2½, 2¾)" from underarm cast-on, ending with a WS row.

Next row: Work pat across 29 (32, 36) sts, k2tog, k2, ssk, k54 (60, 68), k2tog, k2, ssk, pat to end—124 (136, 152) sts. Work 3 rows even. Work Rows 1-6 of Dimple Eyelet pat, keeping first and last 4 sts in border pat as est. Work 2 rows in St st with border edges.

Next row: Work 4 border sts, k25 (28, 32), inc, k1, inc, k55 (61, 69), inc, k1, inc, k30 (33, 37), work 4 border sts—128 (140, 156) sts. Work 2 rows even.

Next row: Work 4 border sts, k26 (29, 33), inc, k1, inc, k57 (63, 71), inc, k1, inc, k31 (34, 38), work 4 border sts—132 (144, 160) sts.

Cont borders in Twisted Garter pat as est, work St st until body measures 5½ (6, 6½)" from underarm cast on, ending with a RS row. Work 5 rows in Twisted Garter pat, binding off on Row 5.

sleeve (make 2)

With RS facing, return sts from waste yarn, dividing onto 3 dpns. Pick up and k2 (2, 3) sts from underarm, place marker (pm), pick up and k2 (2, 3) more sts from underarm, k around Sleeve to marker—47 (52, 59) sts. K 4 rnds. Dec next rnd and every following 8th rnd 5 (6, 6) times more as follows: K1, ssk, k to last 3 sts, k2tog, k1—35 (38, 45) sts rem. Work even until Sleeve measures 6½ (7½, 8)" from underarm. Working flat, work 5 rows in Twisted Garter pat, binding off on Row 5.

Shape Collar

Starting at the Left Front border and working from the WS with circular needle, pick up and k78 (84, 90) sts around neck edge, stopping before Right Front border.

Row 1 (WS): Working first and last 4 sts in Twisted Garter, p across.

Row 2: Working first and last 4 sts in Twisted Garter pat, k across.

Rep these 2 rows until collar measures 2", ending with Row 2. Work 5 rows in Twisted Garter pat, binding off on Row 5.

finishing

Sew snap at center front neck of sweater along Front borders. Cut two 36" lengths of ribbon and weave through eyelets around waist; tie into a bow.

HAT

With 16" circular needle, cast on 84 (96) sts. Work back and forth in Twisted Garter pat for 4 rows for border. Do not turn after row 4. Pm and join; k 1 rnd. Work Rnds 1–6 of Dimple Eyelet pat. Cont in St st until piece measures 3¼ (3¾)" from cast-on edge.

Shape Crown

Next round: (K10, k2tog) around. K 1 rnd. Rep these 2 rnds, working one less stitch before dec with each dec rnd and changing to dp needles when necessary, until you have completed the (k5, k2tog) rnd. From this point forward, omit the plain rnds between dec rnds. Cont to dec every rnd until you have completed the (k2tog) rnd—7 (8) sts rem. Break yarn and draw through rem sts.

finishing

Sew border edges tog.

Cut two 25" lengths of ribbon. Weave ribbon through eyelets around lower edge. Tie upper band of ribbon into a bow on the outside of the hat; tie lower band of ribbon into a knot on inside of hat.

BOOTIES

Note: *Cuff and heel of bootie are worked flat; work is joined into a rnd after the heel is turned.*

Using dpns, cast on 22 sts. Work 4 rows in Twisted Garter pat. P 1 row. Work Rnds 1–6 of Dimple Eyelet pat. K 1 row. Break yarn. Place first 6 sts on waste yarn, rejoin yarn and k next 10 sts (these will become the heel sts), place last 6 sts on waste yarn.

Shape Heel

Working over 10 heel sts, k 9 rows, ending with a WS row.

Turn Heel

Row 1: K5, k2tog, k1; turn.
Row 2: K2, k2tog, k1; turn.
Row 3: K3, k2tog, k1; turn.
Row 4: K4, k2tog, k1—6 heel sts rem.

Shape Gusset

Place 12 sts from waste yarn on one dpn (this will join the cuff of the bootie into a rnd). K3, place marker (pm) for beg of rnd, k3, pick up and k 5 sts along selvedge of heel flap, pm for gusset, k2, ssk, k4, k2tog, k2, pm for other gusset, pick up and k 5 sts along rem heel selvage, k first 3 sts again—26 sts. K to 2 sts before first gusset marker, k2tog, k to next gusset marker, ssk, k to end of rnd.

Next round: K. Rep these 2 rnds until 20 sts rem.

Shape Foot

K around until foot measures approx 2½" from back of heel.

Shape Toe

K3, k2tog, ssk, k6, k2tog, ssk, k3. K16. K2, k2tog, ssk, k4, k2tog, ssk, k2—12 sts. Break yarn and draw through rem sts.

finishing

Cut two 10" lengths of ribbon. Thread ribbon through 2 center front eyelet holes, and tie it in a bow.

Design by Kristen Spurkland

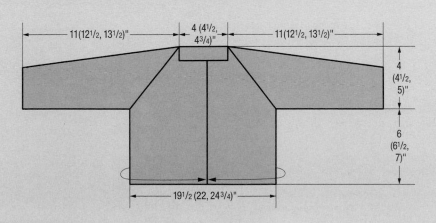

polka-dot jacket & hat

The oversize polka dots make this jacket
and hat combo a real standout. Babies—
and parents, too— will love the feel of
the fluffy yarn.

skill level: Intermediate

sizes: Cardigan: 12 (18, 24) mos.
Hat: S (M, L)
Instructions are written for the smallest size with
changes for larger sizes given in parentheses.
When only one number is given, it applies to
all sizes.
Note: *For ease in working, circle all numbers*
pertaining to the size you are knitting.

finished measurements
Cardigan:
Chest = 24 (26, 28)"
Hat:
Circumference = 17 (18, 19)"

suggested yarns
Lion Brand Polarspun (Art. 360)
100% polyester; 1¾ oz. (50 g);
137 yds. (125 m); chunky weight yarn
● 2 (2, 3) balls #139 Pink (MC)
● 1 (1, 1) ball #100 Snow White (CC)

needles & extras
● Size 9 (5.5 mm) needles OR SIZE NEEDED
  TO OBTAIN GAUGE
● Size 7 (4.5 mm) knitting needles
● Size 9 (5.5 mm) 16" circular knitting needle
● Size 7 (4.5 mm) 16" circular knitting needle
● Size 9 (5.5 mm) double-pointed needles
  (dpns)

● Blunt-end yarn needle
● Five ¾" (19 mm) buttons

gauge
14 sts and 20 rows = 4" (10 cm) in St st using
larger needles.
TAKE TIME TO CHECK YOUR GAUGE.

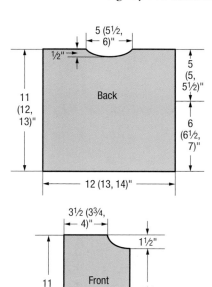

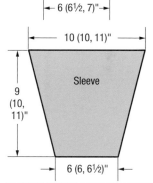

Shape crown

Next rnd: Sl marker, *ssk, k8, pm; rep from * around to marker at beg of rnd. Cont to dec 6 sts every rnd, working ssk after each marker and AT THE SAME TIME, when 48 sts rem, change to CC. When 6 sts rem, cut yarn, run tail through rem sts and fasten off. Weave in ends.

Design by Lisa Carnahan

instructions

CARDIGAN

back

Using smaller needles and MC, cast on 44 (48, 52) sts. K 6 rows. Change to larger needles and work in St st for 1 (1, 1½)", ending with a WS row.

Next row: K3, work chart, *bottom right,* over next 11 sts, k12 (14, 16), work chart over next 11 sts, k to end. Continue working in St st over next 14 rows of chart. Work even until piece measures 6 (6½, 7)" from beg, ending with a WS row.

Next row: K7 (9, 11), work chart over next 11 sts, k12 (14, 16), work chart over next 11 sts, k to end. Work from chart as before, then work even until piece measures 11 (12, 13)", ending with a WS row.

Shape Back Neck

Note: Work all increases and decreases one stitch in from edge.

K14 (15, 16), bind off center 16 (18, 20), k14 (15, 16). Working both shoulders at same time, dec 1 st at each neck edge every row twice. Bind off rem 12 (13, 14) sts.

left front

Using smaller needles and MC, cast on 21 (23, 25) sts. K 6 rows. Change to larger needles and work in St st until piece measures 1 (1, 1½)", ending with a WS row.

Next row: K3, work chart over next 11 sts, k to end. Continue working in St st over next 14 rows following chart. Work even until piece measures 6 (7, 7½)", ending with a WS row.

Next row: K7 (9, 11), work chart over next 11 sts, k to end. Work chart as before, then work even until piece measures 9½ (10½, 11½)", ending with a RS row.

Shape Neck

Bind off 5 (6, 7) sts. Dec 1 st at neck edge every row 4 times—12 (13, 14) sts. Work even until piece measures same as Back. Bind off all sts.

right front

Work as for Left Front, reversing neck shaping.

sleeve (make 2)

Using smaller needles and MC, cast on 21 (21, 23) sts.

K 6 rows. Change to larger needles and work in St st. Inc 1 st on each side every 4th row 4 (2, 2) times, then every 6th row 3 (5, 6) times—35 (35, 39) sts. AT THE SAME TIME, when piece measures ½ (1, 1½)" beyond first 6 Garter st rows, work chart on center 11 sts. Continue in St st until piece measures 5½ (6, 7)", ending with a WS row.

Next row: K to last 14 sts, work chart over next 11 sts, k to end. Work chart over next 14 rows, then continue in MC until Sleeve measures 9 (10, 11)". Bind off loosely.

finishing

Sew shoulder seams.

Shape Neck Band

With RS facing and using smaller circular needle and MC, pick up and k 40 (44, 48) sts around neck edge. K 5 rows. Bind off loosely.

Make Button Band

With RS facing and using smaller needles and MC, pick up and k36 (40, 44) sts along Right Front edge (for boy) or Left Front edge (for girl). K 5 rows. Bind off.

Make Buttonhole Band

With RS facing and using smaller needles and MC, pick up and k36 (40, 44) sts along Right Front edge (for girl) or Left Front edge (for boy). K 2 rows.

Buttonhole Row: K3, *k2tog, yo, k5 (6, 7); rep from * to last 5 sts, k2tog, yo, k3. K 2 rows. Bind off. Mark Front and Back edges 5 (5, 5½)" from shoulder seams. Attach Sleeves between markers. Sew side and underarm seams. Sew buttons onto button band.

HAT

Using smaller circular needle and MC, cast on 60 (63, 66) sts. Place marker (pm) to indicate beg of rnd and join. K 6 rnds. Change to larger needles.

Next rnd: K1, work chart, *bottom right,* over next 11 sts, k9 (10, 11), work chart, k9 (10, 11), work chart, k8 (9, 10). Work even over next 14 rows of chart. Continue until piece measures 4¼ (4½, 5)", decreasing 0 (3, 0) sts on last rnd—60 (60, 66) sts.

skill level: Easy

size: One size fits most toddlers.

finished measurements
Mitten:
Approx 2½×4"
Cap:
Circumference = approx 18"

suggested yarns
Lion Brand Wool-Ease Sportweight (Art. 660)
80% acrylic, 20% wool; 5 oz. (140 g);
435 yds. (398 m); sport weight
● 1 ball #099 Fisherman (MC)

Lion Brand Wool-Ease (Art. 620)
80% acrylic, 20% wool; 3 oz. (85 g);
197 yds. (180 m); worsted weight
● 1 ball #138 Cranberry (CC)

needles & extras
● Size 4 (3.5 mm) knitting needles OR SIZE
   NEEDED TO OBTAIN GAUGE
● Blunt-end yarn needle
● 24" length of narrow off-white ribbon

gauge
24 sts and 32 rows = 4" (10 cm) in St st.
TAKE TIME TO CHECK YOUR GAUGE.

candy cane set

Keep a youngster warm with this sweet striped hat and mitten
set that resembles holiday candy. The fringe ties and dangling
pom-pom add unique detailing.

special abbreviations

Ssk (slip, slip, knit) = Slip next 2 stitches knitwise, one at a time to right-hand needle, insert tip of left-hand needle into the fronts of these 2 stitches and knit them together.

instructions

MITTEN (make 2)

With MC, cast on 30 sts. *Leaving 8" tails when joining colors, with MC, p 1 row, k 1 row, p 1 row. With CC, k 1 row. For stripe pat, rep from * for total of 6 times. Purl 1 row with MC.

Shape top

Row 1: Maintaining stripe pat, (ssk, k11, k2tog) twice.

Row 2: P26.

Row 3: (Ssk, k9, K2tog) twice.

Row 4: P22.

Row 5: (K2tog) across.

Row 6: P11. Leaving a 12" tail, cut yarn. Thread tail into yarn needle and back through rem sts twice.

finishing

Take all tails to outside (RS). Matching the stripes, tie each set of 4 tails together in an overhand knot along the side edge. Trim to ½". Using the tail from the top, sew the seam of the side edge. Let the lower edge roll up naturally.

CAP

Leaving 8" tail, with MC, cast on 120 sts.

Row 1 and each following WS row: Purl across.

Row 2: K28, k2tog, ssk, k56, k 2tog, ssk, k28—116 sts.

Row 4: K27, K2tog, ssk, k54, k2tog, ssk, k27—112 sts.

Rows 6–7: With MC, work even in St st on 112 sts.

Row 8: *K1, yo, k2tog; rep from * across—37 eyelets made.

Row 9: Purl.

Rows 10–19: Work even in St st on 112 sts.

Row 20: With MC, k11, (k2tog, k20) 4 times, k2tog, k11— 107 sts.

Note: When joining new color, leave 8" tails at side edges.

Row 21: With MC, purl.

Row 22: With CC, knit.

Row 23: With MC, purl.

Row 24: With MC, knit.

Row 25: With MC, purl.

Row 26: With CC, knit.

Row 27: With MC, Purl.

Row 28: With MC, (k19, k2tog) five times, k2—102 sts.

Row 29: With MC, purl.

Rows 30–31: Rep Rows 22–23.

Row 32: With MC, (k18, k2tog) times, k2—97 sts.

Row 33: With MC, purl.

Rows 34–35: Rep Rows 22–23.

Row 36: With MC, (k17, k2tog) five times, k2—92 sts.

Row 37: With MC, purl.

Cont in 4-row stripe pat, dec 5 sts evenly spaced on each MC knit row until 12 sts rem.

Next row: K2tog across. P6. Cut yarn, leaving an 8" tail. Thread tail into yarn needle and back through sts. Draw up to close opening. Sew to first stripe row.

finishing

Note: The cap is not sewn together along the opening where the tails are tied together.

Take all tails to outside (RS). Matching stripes and working along the side edge, tie each set of 4 tails tog in an overhand knot. Using beg tail at lower edge, join MC rows up to first stripe. Let this portion roll up naturally. Weave ribbon in the eyelets made in Row 8. Tie ribbon ends together.

pom-pom

Wind CC around a credit card 25 times; tie a separate strand tightly around the center. Carefully remove the card. Cut the ends of the pom-pom. Trim and sew the pom-pom to the tip of the cap.

kids

Kids' sweaters can be bright and bold, practical, and tough enough to withstand the wear and tear of active boys and girls. Knit up one or more of these kid-friendly coverings for the children in your life.

best-friends sweaters

Knit a doll sweater to match one for a little girl. The brightly colored flower is *intarsia*, which means it's knitted right into the pattern. Both sweaters are finished with scallops.

GIRL'S SWEATER
sizes: 4 (6, 8, 10)

skill level: Intermediate
Instructions are written for the smallest size with changes for larger sizes given in parentheses. When only one number is given, it applies to all sizes.
Note: *For ease in working, circle all numbers pertaining to the size you're knitting.*

finished measurements
Chest = 25 (27, 30, 32)"
Length = 13½ (14½, 15½, 17)"
Upper arm = 9½ (10¾, 11¾, 12½)"

suggested yarns
Shepherd/Classic Elite Colour 4 Me
100% Superwash wool; 1¾ oz. (50 g);
98 yd. (89 m); double knitting (DK) weight
● 6 (7, 9, 10) balls #4953 Pink (MC)
● 1 ball #4954 Peri (A)
● 1 ball #4954 Light Green (B)

needles
● Size 6 (4 mm) knitting needles OR SIZE NEEDED TO OBTAIN GAUGE
● Size 4 (3.5 mm) knitting needles
● One extra size 4 (3.5 mm) needle
● Two size 4 (3.25 mm) double-pointed needles (dpns)

gauge
21 sts and 28 rows = 4" (10 cm) in St st using larger needles.
TAKE TIME TO CHECK YOUR GAUGE.

pattern stitch
T-TWIST

K7, then rotate the LH needle counterclockwise 360 degrees, then k another 6 sts and rotate the LH needle again counterclockwise 360 degrees. Continue to k6 sts and rotate LH needle, to end of the row, ending last rep with k7.

instructions
back

Noting that one st at each edge is for selvedge and not reflected on schematics, *with MC, cast on 68 (74, 80, 86) sts. Beg with a k row, work 6 rows in St st. Work T-twist **. Beg with a p row, work 8 rows in St st; leave sts on spare needle. Rep from * to ** for second T-twist. P 1 row.

Join Pieces

With RS facing, place second T-twist over first with needles pointing in same direction. With 3rd needle, k the two pieces tog ***. Cont in St st until piece measures 7 (7½, 8, 9)" from joining, ending with a WS row.

Shape Raglan

Bind off 5 (6, 7, 7) sts at beg of next 2 rows.

Dec row (RS): K2, k2tog, k to last 4 sts, ssk (see Knit Basics, page 48), k2. Purl next row. Rep last 2 rows 13 (15, 17, 19) more times—30 (30, 30, 32) sts. Bind off on next RS row.

front

Work from * to *** as for Back. Beg with a p row, work 27 (35, 43, 53) St st rows.

First chart row: With MC, k30 (33, 36, 39) k4 A, k to end. Following chart, work raglan shaping as for

Back to 1" less than Back, ending with WS row. Place markers each side of center 18 (18, 18, 20) sts.

Next row: Cont raglan shaping and k to marker, join a new ball of yarn and bind off sts bet markers, k to end, dec for raglan. Working sides AT THE SAME TIME with separate balls, dec 1 st each neck edge every row 6 times and cont shaping raglans. Fasten off rem st.

sleeve (make 2)

With MC, cast on 38 (38, 44, 44) sts. Rep from * to *** as for Back. Beg with a purl row, work St st and AT THE SAME TIME, inc 1 st each edge next RS row and every 8th row 4 (0, 3, 3) more times and every 6th row 2 (9, 6, 8) times. Work even on 52 (58, 64, 68) sts to 8 (9, 10½, 12)" above cast-on, ending with a WS row. Shape raglan as for Back. Bind off rem 14 sts.

finishing

Block pieces. Sew Sleeves to Front and Back. Join underarm and side seams.

collar

With MC, cast on 92 (92, 92, 98) sts. Rep from * to ** as for Back. Work 10 rows in St st. Bind off. Join ends to form back neck seam.

With RS tog, pin Collar around neck, matching seam to center of back neck. Sew in place.

leaf (make 2)

With B, cast on 9 sts.

Rows 1, 3, and 5: K3, sl2tog kwise, k1, p2sso, k3—7 sts.

Rows 2 and 4: K1, m1, k2, p1, k2, m1, k1—9 sts.

Row 6: K3, p1, k3.

Row 7: K2, sl2tog kwise, k1, p2sso, k2—5 sts.

Row 8: K2, p1, k2.

Row 9: K1, sl2tog kwise, k1, p2sso, k1—3 sts.

Row 10: K1, p1, k1.

Row 11: Sl2tog kwise, k1, p2sso—1 st. Fasten off.

i-cord

Using dpns and B, cast on 3 sts. *K3, do not turn work, slide 3 sts to end of RH; rep from * until desired length; fasten off.

With pink, make French knots in the center of the daisy (see diagram, *opposite*). Pin the I-cord onto the Front below the flower center and bet the two lower petals. Making the cord form two curves with the first toward the left seam and second toward the right seam, sew it in place. Sew one Leaf to the right of the first curve and the other Leaf to the left of the second curve.

Design by Nicky Epstein

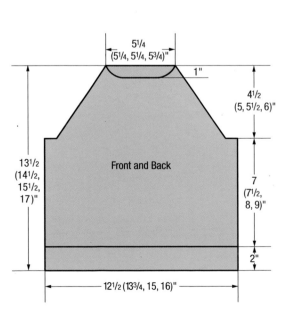

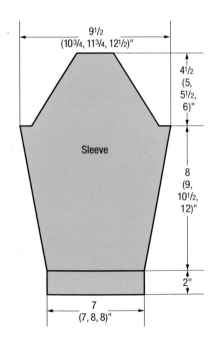

DOLL'S SWEATER
finished measurement
Chess = 5½"

suggested yarns
Anchor Tapestry Wool
100% wool; 11 yds. (10 m); fingering weight
- 4 skeins #8454 Pink (MC)
- 1 skein #8606 Violet (A)
- 1 skein #9096 Lime (B)

needles & extras
- Size 2 (2.75 mm) knitting needles OR SIZE NEEDED TO OBTAIN GAUGE
- Small snap
- Blunt-end yarn needle

gauge
8 sts and 10 rows = 1" in St st.
TAKE TIME TO CHECK YOUR GAUGE.

-  #8606 Violet Lazy Daisy
- · #9096 Lime French Knot
- #9096 Lime Lazy Daisy
- #9096 Lime Stem Stitch

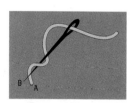

Stem Stitch Diagram   French Knot

body
With MC, cast on 39 sts. K 1 row, p 1 row. *K3, T-twist; rep from * across, ending k3. Cont in St st until piece measures 2½" from beg, ending with a WS row.
Divide for Front and Back
K8 (Left Back), bind off 4 sts (armhole), k 15 (Front); bind off next 4 sts (armhole), k to end (Back).

right back
P8, slip rem sts to a holder. Work 2 rows in St st.
Shape Raglan
K1, ssk, k to end. P 1 row. Rep last 2 rows 3 times more—4 sts. Place sts on a holder.

front
P15 sts from holder, leave rem 8 sts on holder. Work 2 rows in St st .
Shape Raglan
K1, ssk (refer to Knit Basics, page 48), k to last 3 sts, k2tog, k1. P 1 row. Rep last 2 rows 3 more times—7 sts. Place sts on a holder.

left back
P8 sts. Work 2 rows in St st.
Shape Raglan
K to last 3 sts, k 2 tog, k1. P 1 row. Rep last 2 rows 3 more times—4 sts. Place sts on a holder.

sleeve (make 2)
Cast on 12 sts. K 1 row. P 1 row. (K3, T-twist) across. P 1 row. Inc 1 st each side every 4th row 3 times—18 sts. Work even until piece measures 2½" from beg.
Shape Raglan
Bind off 2 sts at beg of next 2 rows—14 sts. K1, ssk, k to last 3 sts, k2tog, k1.
P 1 row. Rep last 2 rows 4 more times—4 sts. Place sts on a holder.

neckband
With RS facing, k across sts from holders, beg with Left Back and inc 4 sts evenly—27 sts. Work in St st for ½", ending with a WS row. Bind off.

finishing
Sew side and sleeve seams. With A, make a lazy daisy on Front, centered about 1½" from top of neckband. With B, add a French knot in center of daisy. With B, stem-stitch the stalk and add a leaf (like one daisy petal) on each side. Sew back seam from lower edge up 1½". Sew snap to top back.

Design by Nicky Epstein

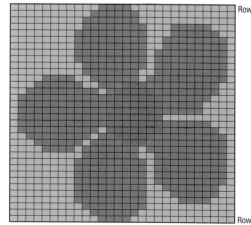

Row 34

Row 1

on the go pullover

It may be a long time before he's ready to drive, but he'll be off to the races in this comfortable pullover. Trimmed with rolled cuffs and hem and accented with button wheels, the sweater knits up quickly in stockinette stitch using chunky-weight yarn.

skill level: Intermediate

sizes: 2 (4, 6, 8)
Instructions are written for the smallest size with changes for larger sizes given in parentheses. When only one number is given, it applies to all sizes.
Note: *For ease in working, circle all numbers pertaining to the size you're knitting.*

finished measurements
Chest = 29 (32, 35, 37)"
Length = 15 (16½, 18, 19½)"

suggested yarns
Lion Brand Wool-Ease Chunky (Art. 630) 80% acrylic, 20% wool; 5 oz. (140 g); 1 53 yds. (140 m); bulky weight
• 2 (3, 3, 4) balls #107 Bluebell (MC)
• 1 (1, 1, 1) ball #133 Pumpkin (CC)

needles & extras
• Size 10½ (6.5 mm) knitting needles OR SIZE NEEDED TO OBTAIN GAUGE
• Size 10 (6 mm) knitting needles
• Size 10 (6 mm) 16" circular knitting needle
• Two 1"-diameter black buttons with four holes for wheels
• Two ring-type stitch markers
• Blunt-end yarn needle

gauge
13½ sts and 16 rows = 4" (10 cm) in St st using larger needles.
TAKE TIME TO CHECK YOUR GAUGE.

instructions

back

Using smaller needles and CC, cast on 49 (55, 59, 63) sts. Beg with a k row, work 10 rows in St st. Change to larger needles.

border

Row 1 (RS): (K1 CC, k1 MC) across, ending with k1 CC.
Row 2: (P1 CC, p1 MC) across, ending with p1 CC. With MC, work even in St st, beg with a k row, until piece measures approx 9½ (10½, 11½, 12½)" from beg, ending with a WS row.

Shape Armholes

Bind off 4 sts at beg of next 2 rows—41 (47, 51, 55) sts. Work even to 15 (16½, 18, 19½)" from beg, ending with a WS row. Bind off loosely.

front

***Notes:** An intarsia car is added to the Front only. While working the chart for St st car, use separate strands of yarn for each color section, bringing the new color from under the previous color to prevent holes. Read the chart from right to left for knit (RS) rows and from left to right for purl (WS) rows.*

Work as for Back until piece measures approx 8½ (10, 10½, 12)" from beg, ending with a WS row and placing markers on either side of 19 center sts for chart placement. Work Car-Motif Chart, *right,* through completion of Row 10, noting armhole shaping will be worked as for Back when piece measures approx 9½ (10½, 11½, 12½)" from beg.
Cont in St st with MC until piece measures approx 12½ (14, 15½, 17)" from beg, ending with a WS row.

Shape Neck

Next row: K16 (19, 20, 22) sts, join a new ball of MC, and bind off center 9 (9, 11, 11) sts; k to end. Working

sides separately and AT THE SAME TIME, bind off 2 sts at each Neck edge once and then 1 st at each edge once. Work even on rem 10 (13, 14, 16) sts for each shoulder to same length as Back, ending with a WS row. Bind off loosely.

sleeve (make 2)

Using smaller needles and CC, cast on 23 (25, 27, 29) sts. Beg with a k row, work 10 rows in St st. Change to larger needles. Work 2 rows of border as for Back. With MC, work in St st, inc 1 st each edge NOW and every 4th row 4 (4, 4, 5) more times, then every 6th row 2 (3, 3, 3) times. Work even on 37 (41, 43, 47) sts until piece measures approx 12 (13½, 14, 15)" from beg, ending with a WS row. Bind off loosely.

finishing

Join shoulder seams. Set in Sleeves, sewing last inch at sides of Sleeve tops to bound-off sts for square armholes. Join underarm and side seams with matching colors.

Shape Neckband

With RS facing and using circular needle and MC, pick up and k21 (21, 23, 23) sts evenly spaced along Back neck and 31 (31, 33, 33) sts evenly spaced along Front neck—52 (52, 56, 56) sts. Place a marker for beg of rnd. Join.
Next 4 rnds: Work rib of k1, p1 around. Change to CC and k 1 rnd.
Next 4 rnds: With CC, work rib of k1, p1 around. Bind off kwise. Turn neckband to inside and sew in place along pick-up rnd.

With CC, sew the buttons in place as wheels using a cross-stitch on each.

Design by Ann E. Smith

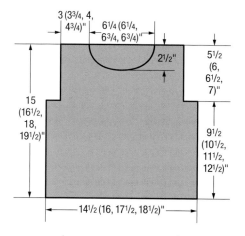

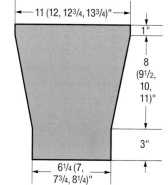

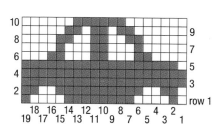

CC (Pumpkin)

little glowworm
cardigan & hat

Worked in easy stockinette stitch, this sweater is accented with bold checked borders. To make the cardigan for a boy, simply change the side of the button band. The hat, worked on a circular needle, includes eyelets, a drawstring, and a lower edge that rolls naturally into a brim.

CARDIGAN
skill level: Easy

sizes: 4 (6, 8, 10)
Instructions are written for the smallest size with changes for larger sizes given in parentheses. When only one number is given, it applies to all sizes.
Note: *For ease in working, circle all numbers pertaining to the size you're knitting.*

finished measurements
Chest (buttoned)= 30½ (32, 34½, 36)"
Length= 16 (18, 20, 22)"

suggested yarn
Muench Bali
50% cotton, 50% acrylic; 1¾ oz. (50 g); 109 yds. (100 m); sport weight
● 4 (5, 6, 7) balls #40 Royal Blue (MC)
● 1 ball #44 Lime (CC)

needles & extras
● Size 5 (3.75 mm) 29" circular knitting needle OR SIZE NEEDED TO OBTAIN GAUGE
● Size 4 (3.5 mm) knitting needles
● Blunt-end yarn needle
● Five JHB International buttons (we used Catty Pillar #22801, size 1⅛")

gauge:
20 sts and 28 rows = 4" (10 cm) in St st using larger needles.
TAKE TIME TO CHECK YOUR GAUGE.

pattern stitches

BORDER (a multiple of 4 sts + 3; a 2-row rep)
Row 1 (WS): With MC, (k3, p1) across, ending k3.
Row 2: With MC, k.
Rep Rows 1–2 for Border pat.

CHECKS (a multiple of 4 sts + 3)
Row 1 (WS): With MC, p.
Row 2: * K3 CC, k1 MC; rep from * across, ending k3 CC.
Row 3: * P3 CC, p1 MC; rep from * across, ending p3 CC.
Row 4: Rep Row 2.
Row 5: Rep Row 1.
Row 6: With MC, k.
Row 7: Rep Row 3.
Row 8: Rep Row 2.
Row 9: Rep Row 3.

instructions

lower body

Notes: *The lower body is worked back and forth in one piece to the armhole, using a circular needle to accommodate the large number of stitches. When working the Checks pat, loosely carry the color not in use along WS of fabric. To change color, bring next strand from under present strand to prevent holes.*
Using the larger needle and MC, cast on 147 (155, 167, 175) sts. Rep Border Rows 1–2 for 3 times total. Rep Checks Rows 1–9 once. With MC and beg with a k row, work in St st until piece measures approx 9 (10½, 12, 13½)" from beg, ending with a WS row.

Shape Armhole

K35 (35, 39, 43); bind off 1 (3, 3, 1) st(s); with 1 st on right needle, k across next 74 (78, 82, 86) sts; bind off 1 (3, 3, 1) st(s); k to end.

left front

Cont in St st on last 35 (35, 39, 43) sts until piece measures approx 14 (16, 18, 20)" from beg, ending with a RS row.

Shape Neck

At beg of neck edge, bind off 5 (5, 8, 11) sts once, 3 sts once, 2 sts once, and 1 st twice. Cont as est on rem 23 (23, 24, 25) sts to approx 16 (18, 20, 22)" from beg, ending with a WS row. Bind off.

back

With the WS facing, join MC and p across 75 (79, 83, 87) sts. Work even to approx 16 (18, 20, 22)" from beg, ending with a WS row. Bind off.

right front

With the WS facing, join MC and p across 35 (35, 39, 43) sts. Reversing neck shaping, work as for Left Front.

sleeve (make 2)

Beg at the cuff with larger needle and MC, cast on 31 (35, 35, 39) sts. Rep Border Rows 1–2 for 3 times total. Rep Checks Rows 1–9 once. With MC, beg St st, inc 1 st each edge every row 2 (2, 0, 0) times, then every 4th row 16 (17, 21, 22) times total—67 (73, 77, 83) sts. Work even to approx 13 (14, 15, 16)" from beg, ending with a WS row. Bind off loosely.

finishing

Join shoulder and sleeve seams. Set in Sleeves.

Neckband

With RS facing and using smaller needles and CC, pick up and k69 (73, 73, 77) sts evenly spaced around neck.

Row 1 (WS): P1; (k3, p1) across.

Row 2: Knit.

Rep Rows 1–2 for 3 more times, then rep Row 1 again. Bind off.

Shape Left Front Band

With the RS facing and using smaller needles and CC, pick up and k84 (95, 100, 117) sts evenly spaced along edge. K9 rows. Bind off.

Shape Right Front Band

With the RS facing and using smaller needles and CC, pick up and k as for Left Band. K3 rows.

Row 4: K10 (9, 10, 11); * bind off 2 sts, k14 (17, 18, 22) more sts—15 (18, 19, 23) sts between buttonholes; rep from * for 5 buttonholes, ending k to end.

Row 5: K across and cast on 2 sts over each buttonhole. K 4 more rows. Bind off. Sew buttons opposite buttonholes. Weave loose ends along WS of fabric.

HAT

skill level: Easy

size: One size fits all.

finished measurement

Circumference = 24"

suggested yarn

Muench Bali
50% cotton, 50% acrylic; 1¾ oz. (50 g); 109 yds. (100 m); sport weight
• 2 balls #44 Lime

needles & extras

• Size 7 (4.5 mm) 16" circular knitting needle
• Size 7 (4.5 mm) double-pointed needles (dpns)
• Ring-type stitch marker
• Blunt-end yarn needle

gauge

16 sts and 24 rnds = 4" (10 cm) using a double strand of yarn.

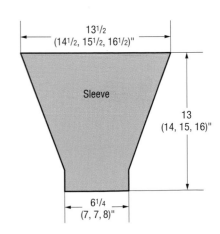

hat

Using a double strand of yarn and circular needle, cast on 96 sts. Join, being careful not to twist the sts. Place a marker to indicate beg of rnd. K 20 rnds.

Eyelet rnd: (K4, yo, k2tog) around. K 20 rnds.

Shape crown

Rnd 1: [(Sl 1 st pwise, k1, pass slipped stitch over k st—skp made), k12, k2tog] 6 times.

Rnd 2: K84.

Rnd 3: (Skp, k10, k2tog) 6 times.

Rnd 4: K72.

Rnd 5: (Skp, k8, k2tog) 6 times.

Rnd 6: K60.

Rnd 7: (Skp, k6, k2tog) 6 times.

Rnd 8: K48. Change to dpns. Arrange sts onto dpns with 16 sts on each of 3.

Rnd 9: (Skp, k4, k2tog) 6 times.

Rnd 10: K36.

Rnd 11: (Skp, k2, k2tog) 6 times.

Rnd 12: K24.

Rnd 13: (Skp, k2tog) 6 times.

Rnd 14: K12.

Rnd 15: (K2tog) 6 times—6 sts rem. Cut yarn, leaving an 8" tail. Thread tail into yarn needle and back through rem 6 sts. Secure tail on WS of fabric.

tie

Using a double strand of yarn, cast on 135 sts. Bind off.

Thread Tie through the eyelets; try on child; tie to fit. Let lower edge roll naturally.

Design by Ann E. Smith

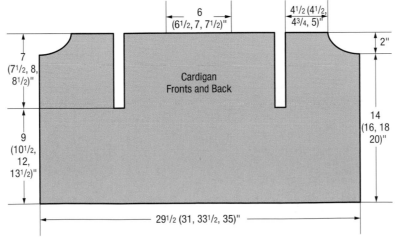

6
(6½, 7, 7½)"

4½ (4½, 4¾, 5)"

2"

7 (7½, 8, 8½)"

Cardigan
Fronts and Back

14 (16, 18 20)"

9 (10½, 12, 13½)"

29½ (31, 33½, 35)"

13½ (14½, 15½, 16½)"

Sleeve

13 (14, 15, 16)"

6¼ (7, 7, 8)"

colorful pullover

This cotton/acrylic pullover is worked in three colors with only two colors on each row. Highlights on the bandings accent the color of the narrow background stripe.

skill level: Intermediate

sizes: 6 (8, 10, 12)
Instructions are written for the smallest size with changes for larger sizes in parentheses. When only one number is given, it applies to all sizes.
Note: *For ease in working, circle all numbers pertaining to the size you're knitting.*

finished measurements
Chest = 32 (34, 36, 38)"
Length = 16 (17, 18, 19)"

suggested yarns
Lion Brand Cotton-Ease
50% cotton, 50% acrylic; 3½ oz (100 g);
207 yds. (188 m); worsted weight
- 1 (1, 2, 2) ball(s) #133 Orangeade (A)
- 2 (2, 3, 3) balls #113 Cherry Red (B)
- 2 (2, 3, 3) balls #158 Pineapple (C)

needles & extras
- Size 7 (4.5 mm) knitting needles OR SIZE NEEDED TO OBTAIN GAUGE
- Size 6 (4.25 mm) knitting needles
- Size 6 (4.25 mm) circular knitting needle
- Blunt-end yarn needle

gauge
17 sts and 24 rows = 4" (10 cm) in Body pat using larger needles.
TAKE TIME TO CHECK YOUR GAUGE.

pattern stitch

K2 P2 RIB (a multiple of 4 sts + 2; a 2-row rep)

Row 1 (RS): * K2, p2; Rep from * across, ending row with k2.

Row 2: * P2, k2; Rep from * across, ending row with p2.

Repeat Rows 1–2.

instructions

back

Beg at lower edge and with smaller needles and Color A, cast on 70 (74, 78, 82) sts. Change to Color B. Work K2 P2 Rib pat, using B only, to approx 1½(2, 2, 2)" from beg, ending with a WS row.

Body Pattern

Change to larger needles, beg Colorful Pattern (see chart, *below*), and work even to approx 16 (17, 18, 19)" from beg, ending with a WS row.

Shape Shoulder

Bind off 8 (8, 9, 9) sts at beg of next 4 rows. Bind off 7 (9, 8, 10) sts at beg of next 2 rows. Bind off rem 24 (24, 26, 26) sts.

front

Work as for Back until piece measures approx 15 (16, 17, 18)" from beg, ending with a WS row.

Shape Neck

Work in pattern from chart across first 29 (31, 32, 34) sts; join new strands and bind off center 12 (12, 14, 14) sts; work to end of row. Work both sides AT ONCE with separate strands of yarn and bind off 3 sts at each neck edge once, then bind off 2 sts at each neck edge once. Dec 1 st at each neck edge once—23 (25, 26, 28) sts rem. Complete as for Back.

sleeve (make 2)

Beg at lower edge and using smaller needles and color A, cast on 30 sts. Change to color B. Work K2 P2 Rib pat, using B only, to approx 1½ (2, 2, 2)" from beg, ending with a WS row and AT THE SAME TIME inc 4 sts evenly across last row—34 sts.

Body Pattern

Change to larger needles, and beg Colorful Pattern for 2 rows. Beg with next RS row, including new sts into pattern as they accumulate, inc at each edge every 4th row 3 (9, 11, 13) times, then every 6th row 9 (5, 4, 3) times—58 (62, 64, 66) sts. Work even to approx 13½ (14, 14½, 15)" from beg, ending with a WS row. Bind off loosely in pat.

finishing

Join shoulder seams.

Neckband

With RS facing and using circular needle and B, pick up and k 64 (64, 68, 68) sts around neckline. Work rnds of K2 P2 Rib pat until band measures approx 1" from beg. Change to A and work one more rnd as you bind off in rib. Place markers 6¾ (7¼, 7½, 7¾)" down from shoulders. Set in Sleeves between markers. Sew underarm and side seams.

Design by Melissa Leapman

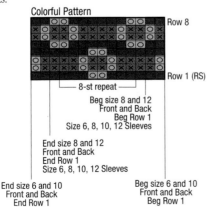

Colorful Pattern

Row 8

Row 1 (RS)

8-st repeat

Beg size 8 and 12
Front and Back
Beg Row 1
Size 6, 8, 10, 12 Sleeves

End size 8 and 12
Front and Back
End Row 1
Size 6, 8, 10, 12 Sleeves

End size 6 and 10
Front and Back
End Row 1

Beg size 6 and 10
Front and Back
Beg Row 1

KEY

A - Orangeade

B - Cherry Red

C - Pineapple

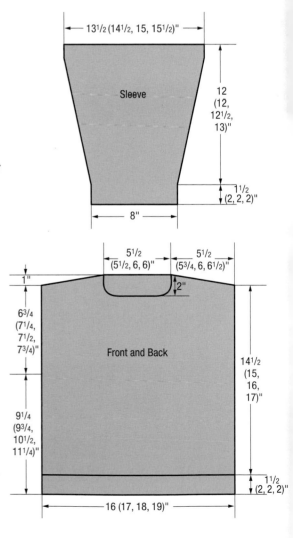

13½ (14½, 15, 15½)"

Sleeve

12 (12, 12½, 13)"

1½ (2, 2, 2)"

8"

5½ (5½, 6, 6)"

5½ (5¾, 6, 6½)"

1"

2"

6¾ (7¼, 7½, 7¾)"

Front and Back

14½ (15, 16, 17)"

9¼ (9¾, 10½, 11¼)"

1½ (2, 2, 2)"

16 (17, 18, 19)"

patchwork
pullover

The minimal shaping
required for this bright
blockbuster makes it a
perfect project for beginning
knitters ready to take their
skills up a notch.

patchwork pullover

skill level: Beginner

sizes: 2 (4, 6, 8)
Instructions are written for the smallest size with changes for larger sizes given in parentheses. When only one number is given, it applies to all sizes.
Note: *For ease in working, circle all numbers pertaining to the size you're knitting.*

finished measurements
Chest = 27½ (29½, 31½, 34)"

suggested yarns
Lion Brand Micro Spun (Art. 910) 100% microfiber acrylic; 2½ oz. (71 g); 168 yds. (154 m); sport weight
● 3 balls #113 Cherry Red (A)
● 2 balls #148 Turquoise (B)
● 2 balls #158 Buttercup (C)
● 2 balls #186 Mango (F)
● 1 ball #147 Purple (D
● 1 ball #194 Lime (E)

needles & extras
● Size 5 (3.75 mm) knitting needles OR SIZE NEEDED TO OBTAIN GAUGE
● Size 4 (3.5 mm) 16" circular knitting needle
● Stitch holders
● Blunt-end yarn needle

gauge
23 sts and 29 rows = 4" (10 cm) over St st using larger needles.
TAKE TIME TO CHECK YOUR GAUGE.

instructions

back
Using larger needles and A, cast on 80 (86, 92, 98) sts and work in St st until piece measures 15½, (16½, 17½, 18½)" from beg. Bind off 23 (25, 28, 29) sts, place center 34 (36, 36, 40) sts on holder for back neck, bind off rem 23 (25, 28, 29) sts.

left front bottom
Using larger needles and B, cast on 41 (44, 47, 50) sts and work even in St st until piece measures 7¾ (8¼, 8¾, 9¼)". Bind off all sts.

right front bottom
With C, work as for Left Front Bottom.

left front top
Using larger needles and D, work as for Left Front Bottom until piece measures 5¾ (6¼, 6¾, 7¼)", ending with a RS row.
Shape Neck
Bind off 8 (9, 9, 11) sts at beg of next row; continue to bind off at beg of neck edge 5 sts once, 3 sts once, 1 st twice. Work even until piece measures same length as Left Front Bottom, bind off rem 23 (25, 28, 29) sts for shoulder.

right front top
With E, work as for Left Front Top, reversing all shaping.

left back sleeve
Notes: *Work all increases 1 stitch in from edge.*
With C, cast on 23 (25, 26, 27) sts and work even for 1", ending with a WS row.
Next row: Inc 1 st at beg of next and every following 4th row 12 (10, 8, 9) more times, then every following

6th row 3 (5, 7, 8) times—39 (41, 42, 45) sts. Work even until piece measures 11½ (12, 12½, 13½)" from beg. Bind off all sts.

left front sleeve

With F, cast on 23 (25, 26, 27) sts and work even for 1", ending with a WS row.

Next row: Inc 1 st at end of next and every following 4th row 12 (10, 8, 9) more times, then every following 6th row 3 (5, 7, 8) times—39 (41, 42, 45) sts. When piece measures same length as Left Back Sleeve, bind off all sts.

right front sleeve

With B, work as for Left Back Sleeve.

right back sleeve

With F, work as for Left Front Sleeve.

finishing

Block all pieces. With WS tog, reverse seam tog (bring edges to RS) Left and Right Front Tops, then Left and Right Front Bottoms, sew tops to bottoms. Reverse seam tog tops of sleeve pieces. Use regular seaming method to sew tog shoulders, sew Sleeves to body, and sew sides of body and underside of Sleeves.

Neck Ribbing

With RS facing and using circular needle and A, and starting at Left shoulder seam, pick up and knit 82 (84, 84, 94) sts evenly around neck, including 34 (36, 36, 40) sts from back neck holder. Work in k1, p1 rib for ¾". Bind off all sts loosely in rib. With reverse seaming, sew tog Left Front and Back Sleeves, then Right Front and Back Sleeves. Place markers on Front and Back 6½(7, 7, 7½)" down from shoulders and sew in Sleeves between markers. Using regular seaming method, sew side and sleeve seams. Using blunt-end yarn needle and A, work overcast embroidery stitch (see diagram, *below*) over exposed (reversed) seams on Body Front and sleeve tops.

Design by Rebecca Rosen

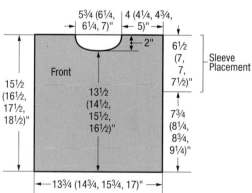

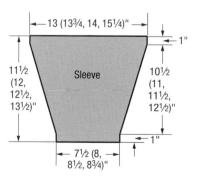

rainbow cardigan &
blueberry bouclé pullover

The cardigan is worked in one piece to the armholes; then divided for the fronts and back; super bulky-weight yarns speeds the project. The pullover pairs blue bouclé yarn with lime green to form a subtle stripe pattern. The wrists, neck, and waist are banded in ribbing.

rainbow cardigan

skill level: Easy

sizes: 18 mos. (2, 3, 4 years)
Instructions are written for the smallest size with changes for larger numbers given in parentheses. When only one number is given, it applies to all sizes.
Note: *For ease in working, circle all numbers pertaining to the size you're knitting.*

finished measurements
Chest (buttoned) = 24 (26, 28, 30)"
Length = 13 (14, 15, 16)"

suggested yarn
Lion Brand Jiffy Thick & Quick (Art. 430)
100% acrylic; 5 oz. (140 g); 84 yds. (76 m);
super bulky weight
• 3 (4, 4, 5) balls #209 Catskills

needles & extras
• Size 15 (10 mm) knitting needles OR SIZE NEEDED TO OBTAIN GAUGE.
• Size 15 (10 mm) 24" circular needle
• Five ¾"-diameter buttons
• Stitch markers
• Blunt-end yarn needle

gauge
8 sts and 16 rows = 4" (10 cm) over Garter st.
TAKE TIME TO CHECK YOUR GAUGE.

instructions

Note: Body is worked in one piece to armholes, then divided for fronts and back.

body

Using circular needle, cast on 46 (50, 54, 58) sts. Work 3 rows in k1, p1 ribbing. Work in Garter st (knit every row) until piece measures 7 (8, 8½, 9)" from beg, ending with a WS row.

Divide for Underarms

K8 (9, 9, 10) sts and place on holder for Right Front, bind off 6 (6, 8, 8) sts for Underarm, k18 (20, 20, 22) sts for Back and place on holder, bind off 6 (6, 8, 8) sts for Underarm, k8 (9, 9, 10) for Left Front.

Shape Left Front

Cont in Garter st on 8 (9, 9, 10) sts for Left Front until armhole measures 4 (3½, 3½, 4)", ending at Front edge.

Shape Neck

Bind off 2 (2, 3, 3) sts at Front edge of next row, then dec 1 st at neck edge on next 2 rows—4 (5, 4, 5) sts rem. Work even until armhole measures 6 (6, 6½, 7)". Bind off 4 (5, 4, 5) shoulder sts.

Shape Back

With WS facing, join yarn to 18 (20, 20, 22) Back sts and work even in Garter st until armhole measures 6 (6, 6½, 7)". Bind off.

Shape Right Front

With WS facing, join yarn to 8 (9, 9, 10) Right Front sts and work as for Left Front.

sleeve (make 2)

Using straight needles, cast on 13 (13, 14, 15) sts. Beg with a k row, work 3 rows in St st for cuff.

Next row (WS): Knit, inc 1 (1, 0, 1) st in center of row—14 (14, 14, 16) sts.
Cont in Garter st, inc 1 st each end of next and every 4th row 1 (1, 2, 2) time(s), then every 6th row 3 times—24 (24, 26, 28) sts. Work even until piece measures 9 (9¾, 10½, 11)" with cuff rolled. Bind off all sts.

finishing

Sew shoulder seams.

Buttonhole Band

With RS facing, pick up and k21 (22, 23, 26) sts along Right Front edge for girls or Left Front edge for boys.
Buttonhole row (WS): K1 (2, 2, 1), [k2tog, yo, k2 (2, 2, 3)] 5 times, k0 (0, 1, 0). K 1 row. Bind off.

Button Band

With RS facing, pick up and k21 (22, 23, 26) sts along Left Front edge for girls or Right Front edge for boys. Knit 2 rows. Bind off.

Neckband

With RS facing, pick up and k5 (6, 6, 6) sts along Right Front band and up front neck edge, 10 (10, 12, 12) sts across back neck edge and 5 (6, 6, 6) sts down Left Front neck edge and buttonhole band—20 (22, 24, 24) sts. Beg with a p row, work 3 rows in St st. Bind off loosely.

Place markers 1½ (1½, 2, 2)" down from top of Sleeves on each side. Sew sleeve seams to markers, leaving rolled edge of cuffs unsewn. Sew in Sleeves, placing rows above markers along bound-off sts of Front and Back to form square armholes. Sew buttons on button band.

Design by Traci Bunkers

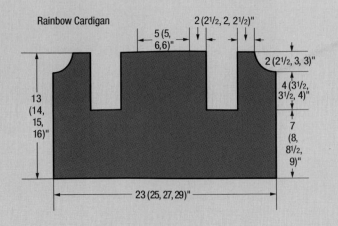

Rainbow Cardigan

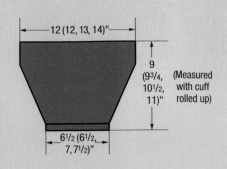

(Measured with cuff rolled up)

blueberry bouclé pullover

skill level: Easy

sizes: 4 (6, 8)
Instructions are written for the smallest size with changes for larger numbers given in parentheses. When only one number is given, it applies to all sizes.
Note: *For ease in working, circle all numbers pertaining to the size you're knitting.*

finished measurements
Chest = 28 (32, 36)"
Length = 15 (16, 18)"

suggested yarn
Lion Brand Bouclé (Art. 930)
79% acrylic, 20% wool, 1% nylon; 2½ oz.
(70 g); 57 yds. (52 m); super bulky weight
• 5 (5, 6) balls #106 Blueberry (MC)
• 2 (2, 2) balls #202 Lime Blue (A)

needles & extras
• Size 10½ (6.5 mm) knitting needles OR SIZE NEEDED TO OBTAIN GAUGE
• Size 10 (6 mm) knitting needles
• Size 10 (6 mm) 16" circular needle
• Stitch markers
• Blunt-end yarn needle

gauge
12 sts and 18 rows = 4" (10 cm) over St st with larger needles.
TAKE TIME TO CHECK YOUR GAUGE.

pattern stitches

1x1 RIBBING (multiple of 2 sts + 1; 2-row rep)
Row 1 (RS): (K1, p1) across; end k1.
Row 2: (P1, k1) across; end p1.
Rep Rows 1 and 2 for 1×1 Ribbing pat.

STRIPE

Beg with a knit row and A, work 4 rows in St st. Beg with a knit row and MC, work 4 rows in St st. Rep last 8 rows for Stripe pat.

instructions

back

Using smaller needles and MC, cast on 41 (47, 53) sts. Work 1½" in 1×1 Ribbing pat, ending with a WS row and inc 1 st in center of last row—42 (48, 54) sts. Change to larger needles and beg with a knit row, work 2 rows in St st. Work 20 rows in Stripe pat. Cont with MC only until piece measures 8½ (9, 10)" from beg, ending with a p row.

Shape Armholes

Bind off 4 (4, 5) sts at beg of next 2 rows—34 (40, 44) sts. Work even until armhole measures 5½ (6, 7)", ending with a p row.

Shape Neck

Next row (RS): K12 (14, 15), join 2nd ball of yarn and bind off center 10 (12, 14) sts; k to end. Working both sides at the same time with separate balls, dec 1 st at each neck edge on next 4 rows—8 (10, 11) sts rem for each shoulder. Work even until armhole measures 6½ (7, 8)", ending with a p row. Bind off.

front

Work as for Back until armhole measures 4½ (5, 6)", ending with a p row.

Shape Front Neck

Next row (RS): K13 (16, 17), join 2nd ball of yarn and bind off center 8 (8,10) sts; k to end. Working both sides at the same time with separate balls, dec 1 st at each neck edge on next 5 (6, 6) rows—8 (10, 11) sts. Cont even until armhole measures 6½ (7, 8)" ending with a p row. Bind off.

sleeve (make 2)

Using smaller needles and MC, cast on 19 (21, 24) sts. Work 1½" in 1×1 Ribbing pat, ending with a WS row. Change to larger needles and work in Stripe pat for 20 rows, and AT THE SAME TIME inc 1 st on each edge on 5th and every 4th row 3 (4, 5) times, every 6th row 6 (6, 0) times, then every 8th row 0 (0, 6) times—39 (43, 48) sts. Cont with MC only until Sleeve measures 13 (14, 15)" from beg, ending with a p row. Bind off. Place markers (pm) on side edges of each Sleeve 1¼ (1¼, 1½)" down from bound-off edge.

finishing

Block to measurements. Join shoulder seams.
Shape Neckband

With RS facing and using circular needle and A, and beg at left shoulder seam, pick up and k58 (60, 64) sts around neck opening. Pm, join, and work 1" in 1×1 Ribbing pat. Bind off loosely in pat. Sew in Sleeves, placing the rows above the markers along bound-off sts of Front and Back to form square armholes. Sew side and sleeve seams. Weave in loose ends.

Design by Shanta Moitran

Blueberry Bouclé Pullover

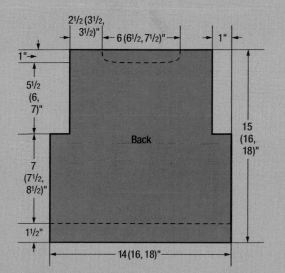

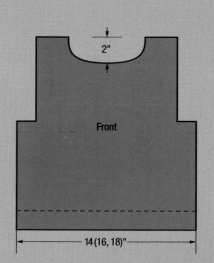

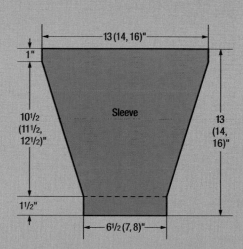

striped sweater with flowers

A self-striping yarn makes this an easy project for beginners. Jumbo snaps provide the closings, and giant yarn-posy flowers mimic buttons.

skill level: Easy

sizes: 4 (6, 8, 10)
Instructions are written for the smallest size with changes for larger sizes given in parentheses. When only one number is given, it applies to all sizes.
Note: *For ease in working, circle all numbers pertaining to the size you're knitting.*

finished measurements
Chest (buttoned) = 30 (32, 34, 36)"
Length = 14 (15½, 17½, 18½)"
Upper arm = 10 (11, 12, 13)"

suggested yarns
Reynolds Santana
55% cotton, 45% acrylic; 1¾ oz. (50 g); 102 yds. (93 m), worsted weight
• 5 (6, 7, 7) balls #16 Multicolor (MC)

Reynolds Saucy Sport
100% mercerized cotton; 1¾ oz. (50 g); 123 yds. (112 m); sport weight
• 1 ball #417 Rose (CC)

needles & extras
• Size 7 (4.5 mm) knitting needles
• Size 8 (5 mm) knitting needles OR SIZE TO OBTAIN GAUGE
• Size 3 (3.25 mm) knitting needles (for flowers)
• Two jumbo snaps
• Blunt-end yarn needle

gauge
16 sts and 26 rows = 4" (10 cm) over St st using larger needles.
TAKE TIME TO CHECK YOUR GAUGE.

instructions

back

Using smaller needles and MC, cast on 60 (64, 68, 72) sts. Beg with a p row, work 6 rows in St st. Changing to larger needles and beg with a p row, cont in St st to 9 (10, 11½, 12)" from beg, end with a WS row.
Shape Armholes
Bind off 7 (8, 9, 10) sts at beg of next 2 rows—46 (48, 50, 52) sts. Work even to 13 (14½, 16½, 17½)" from beg, ending with a RS row.
Shape Neckband
Next row (WS): P10, k26 (28, 30, 32) sts, p10.
Next row (RS): Knit.
Rep last 2 rows twice more, then rep WS row again. Bind off.

right front

With smaller needles and MC, cast on 32 (34, 36, 38) sts.
Row 1 (WS): P to last 5 sts, k5.
Row 2: Knit.
Rep last 2 rows twice more. Change to larger needles and cont est pat until piece from beg measures same as Back to underarm, ending with a RS row.
Shape Armhole
Bind off 7 (8, 9, 10) sts—25 (26, 27, 28) sts.
Shape Neck
Work even to 11 (12½, 14½, 15½)" from beg, ending with a RS row.
Next row (WS): P10, k15 (16, 17, 18).
Next row: Knit across.
Rep last 2 rows twice more, then rep WS row again. Bind off 10 (11, 12, 13) sts, k to end.
Next row (WS): P10, k5.
Next row (RS): Knit.
Rep last 2 rows until piece measures same length as Back, ending with WS row. Bind off.

left front

Using smaller needles and MC, cast on 32 (34, 36, 38) sts.
Row 1 (WS): K5, p to end.
Row 2: Knit.
Rep last 2 rows twice more. Change to larger needles and cont est pat until piece measures same as Back to underarm, ending with a WS row.
Shape Armhole
Bind off 7 (8, 9, 10) sts—25 (26, 27, 28) sts.
Shape Neck
Work even to same length as Right Front to neck, ending with a RS row.
Next row (WS): K15 (16, 17, 18), p10.
Next row: Knit across.
Rep last 2 rows twice more, then rep WS row again. K15, bind off 10 (11, 12, 13) sts. With WS facing, rejoin yarn at neck edge, k5, p10. Complete as for Right Front.

sleeve (make 2)

Using smaller needles and MC, cast on 26 (28, 30, 32) sts. Beg with a p row, work 7 rows in St st. Change to larger needles. Inc 1 st each edge now and every 8th row 6 (7, 8, 9) times more. Work even on 40 (44, 48, 52) sts to 11¾ (13, 14¾, 16½)" from beg, ending with a WS row. Bind off loosely.

finishing

Join shoulder seams. Set in Sleeves, sewing last 1¾ (2, 2¼, 2½)" each side of sleeve edge to bound-off sts from armholes. Join underarm and side seams. Sew the first snap ¼" from neckband bind-off and the second 1½" below the first. Sew mates on opposite front band to match.

flower (make 2)

See instructions on page 44. Place a flower just below each snap on Right Front; take tails to back and tie them into several overhand knots.

Design by Ann E. Smith

making posies

1. Leaving an 8" tail, cast on 30 sts. P 1 row. (K4; turn) 12 times.

2. *Bind off 6 sts, k3 additional sts—4 sts; turn. (K4; turn) 11 times. Rep from * across, ending last rep with bind-off of rem sts—5 petals.

3. Leaving an 8" tail, cut yarn. Thread tail into a blunt-end yarn needle and back through cast-on sts. Pull up to close opening. Stitch from side to side in the inside circle to further close the opening. Take tail to WS of flower. Tie tails tog and use the ties to attach the flower.

4. The finished posy is ready to attach to the sweater.

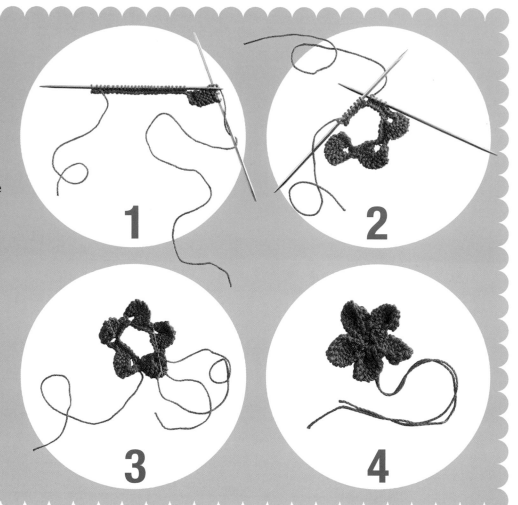

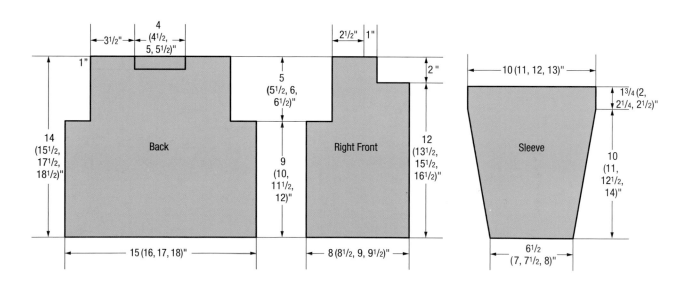

knitbasics

abbreviations

The abbreviations used throughout this book—plus other common ones—are listed below.

approx	approximately
beg	begin(ning)(s)
cn	cable needle
cont	continued or continuing
dec	decrease(s)(ing)
dpn(s)	double-pointed needle(s)
est	established
foll	follow(s)(ing)
inc	increase(s)(ing)
k or K	knit
kwise	as if to knit
k2tog	knit two stitches together
M1	make one stitch
p or P	purl
pat	pattern
pm	place marker
psso	pass slipped stitch over
p2sso	pass two slipped stitches over
p2tog	purl two stitches together
pwise	as if to purl
rem	remain(s)(ing)
rep	repeat(s)(ing)
rnd(s)	round(s)
RS	right side(s) of work
sl	slip
sm	slip marker

ssk	(slip, slip, knit) slip two stitches, one at a time knitwise, insert left needle and knit two together
ssp	(slip, slip, purl) slip two stitches, one at a time knitwise, pass back to left needle, purl together through back loops
st(s)	stitch(es)
St st	stockinette stitch (knit 1 row, purl 1row)
tbl	through the back loop(s)
tog	together
WS	wrong side of work
wyib	with yarn in back
wyif	with yarn in front
yo	yarn over
yon	yarn over needle
yrn	yarn around needle
( )	work instructions within parentheses in the place directed and the number of times indicated
[ ]	work step in brackets the number of times indicated
*	repeat the instructions following the asterisk as directed

slip knot

Leaving a 6" tail, use your right hand to wrap the yarn clockwise around the index and middle fingers of your left hand, then drop the yarn strand behind those two fingers as shown in illustration 1, *below*; let your middle finger slip away from the work and pull the strand of yarn through the middle of the circle, forming a loop.

Place the loop on the needle and gently tug on the two strands to shape the knot (see illustration 2, *below*). The slip knot counts as the first cast-on stitch. For practice, take the slip knot off the needle and make it two or three more times. Once you've mastered the slip knot, try the cast-on methods that follow on page 46.

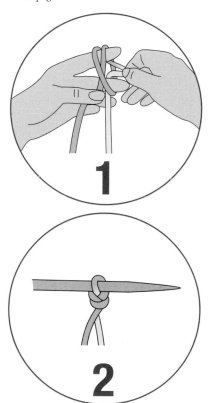

choosing your yarn

You've chosen your pattern and plan to make it just as it appears in the photograph. No problem. But what happens when you get to the yarn store and see all those fabulous yarns? You just might be tempted to make a change.

If you'd like to use other yarns for the projects shown, use the information provided about the yarn shown and purchase one ball of yarn in a similar weight; then make a gauge swatch with it (see page 46). When you have the correct gauge, you're safe to buy the rest of the yarn for your project—make sure you have enough yardage with the new yarn.

long tail cast-on

Estimate a yarn tail length that is three times the width of what the cast-on edge will be.

Step 1 Make a slip knot this distance from the yarn end and place it on the right-hand needle.

Step 2 *Position the thumb and index finger of your left hand between the two strands of yarn. Secure the yarn tails by closing your other fingers around the tails into the palm of your hand.

Step 3 Moving in an upward direction, insert the needle under the yarn on the thumb and into the loop that's formed around the thumb. Take the needle over the top of the yarn in front of the index finger and guide it down into the thumb loop—the strand of yarn from the index finger easily moves along with the needle. Pull the strand through the thumb loop, making a new loop on the right needle.

Step 4 Drop the yarn around the thumb, and spread your index finger and thumb to tighten the loop on the needle— one cast-on stitch is made. Repeat from * to make a second cast-on stitch.

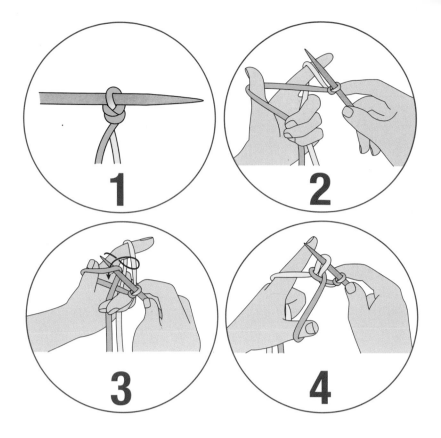

cable cast-on

Step 1 Make a slip knot on the left needle.

Step 2 Insert the right needle through the slip knot and pass the yarn over the right needle. Pull a loop through and place this loop on the left needle.

Step 3 Insert the right needle between the last two stitches on the left needle. Pass yarn over the right needle. Draw a loop through and place the loop on the left needle. Continue adding loops as established until you have the desired number.

making a gauge swatch

Using the recommended needles and yarn, cast on a few more stitches than the number indicated by the gauge printed on the yarn band for 4" (10 cm). Work the pattern for at least 4". Loosely bind off or remove the swatch from the needles. Place a ruler over the swatch; count the number of stitches across 1" and the number of rows down 1", including fractions of stitches or rows. If you have too many stitches and rows, switch to larger needles; if you have too few stitches, use smaller needles.

grafting stockinette stitches

Hold wrong sides together with the needles pointed to the right. Thread the yarn tail into a yarn needle. *Insert the yarn needle knitwise through the first stitch on the front needle and let the stitch drop from the needle.

Insert the yarn needle into the second stitch on the front needle purlwise and pull the yarn through, leaving the stitch on the needle.

Insert the yarn needle into the first stitch on the back needle purlwise and let it drop from the needle. Insert the yarn needle knitwise through the second stitch on the back needle and pull the yarn through, leaving the stitch on the needle. Repeat from * across until all stitches have been joined. Adjust the tension as necessary. Weave in loose ends.

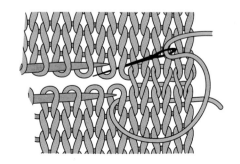

knit stitch

STEP 1 With yarn in back, insert the right-hand needle from front to back into the first stitch on the left-hand needle. Notice that the right-hand needle is behind the left-hand needle.

STEP 2 Form a loop by wrapping the yarn under and around the right-hand needle.

STEP 3 Pull the loop through the stitch so the loop is in front of the work.

STEP 4 Slip the first or "old" knit stitch over and off the tip of the left-hand needle, leaving it on the right-hand needle.

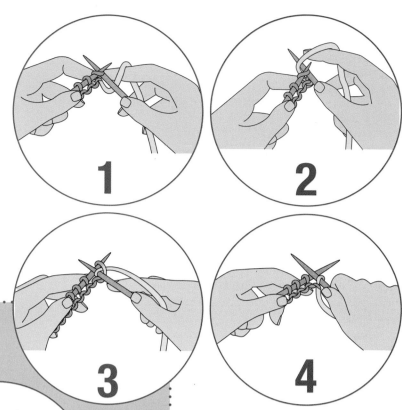

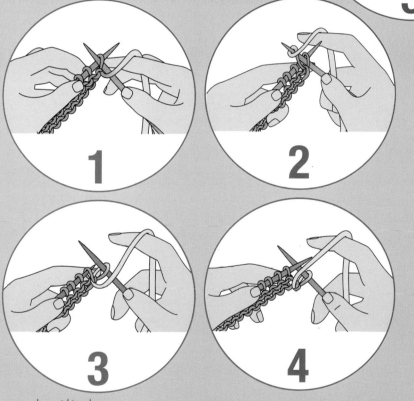

purl stitch

STEP 1 With yarn in front of the work, put the right-hand needle from back to front into the first stitch on the left-hand needle.

STEP 2 Form a loop by wrapping the yarn on top of and around the right-hand needle.

STEP 3 Pull the loop through the stitch to make a new purl stitch.

STEP 4 Slip the first or "old" purl stitch over and off the tip of the left-hand needle, leaving it on the right-hand needle.

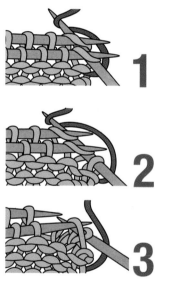

3-needle bind-off

With RS together, hold in your left hand two needles with an equal number of stitches on each and with points facing to the right.

STEP 1 Using a third needle of the same size, knit together one stitch from each needle.

STEPS 2 & 3 *Knit together the next stitch from each needle, pass the first stitch worked over the second stitch to bind off; repeat from * across to bind off all stitches.

specialty stitches

INCREASING STITCHES

• M1 = make one (version A)

increased stitch slants to the right on right side of fabric

Insert the tip of the left needle from back to front under the strand that lies between the next stitch on the left needle and the last stitch worked on the right needle. See the illustration at *right*.

Referring to the illustration at *far right*, insert the right needle from left to right into the front loop of the lifted strand, and knit it from this position.

• M1 = make one (version B)

increased stitch slants to the left on right side of fabric

Insert the tip of the left needle from front to back under the strand that lies between the first stitch on the left needle and the last stitch worked on the right needle. See the illustration at *right*.

Referring to the illustration at *far right*, knit the strand on the left needle, inserting the needle from right to left into the back loop.

Note: *You also can increase by knitting into the front and back of a single stitch. The M1 versions do not leave holes in your fabric.*

DECREASING STITCHES

• ssk = slip, skip, knit

decreased stitch slants to the left on right side of fabric

As if to knit, slip the first two stitches from the left needle one at a time to the right needle as shown at *right*.

Insert the left needle into these two stitches from back to front as shown at *far right*, and knit them together from this position.

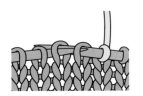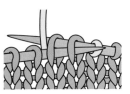

• k2tog = knit two together

decreased stitch slants to the right on right side of fabric

Working from left to right at the point of the decrease, insert the tip of the right needle into the second and then the first stitch on the left needle; knit the two stitches together as shown in the illustration at *right*.

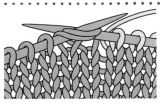

• p2tog = purl two together

decreased stitch slants to the right on right side of fabric

Working from right to left at the point of the decrease, insert the tip of the right needle into the first two stitches on the left needle and purl the two stitches together. See the illustration at *right*.

making a pom-pom

Wind yarn around a piece of cardboard or the palm of your hand loosely 100 times. Tie a 10" strand tightly around all the loops. Cut the yarn bundle opposite the tied end. Leaving the tails free, trim the pom-pom so that it is rounded and measures 1–2" in diameter. Tie onto piece with tails; trim tails.

for more help

Visit www.yarnstandards.com for downloadable knitting information compiled by the Craft Yarn Council of America. You'll find standard sizing information, abbreviations, yarn weights and sizes, and more—all valuable data for knitters.